JBoss Portal Server Development

Create dynamic, feature-rich, and robust enterprise portal applications

Ramanujam Rao

BIRMINGHAM - MUMBAI

JBoss Portal Server Development

First published: January 2009

Production Reference: 1190109

Published by Packt Publishing Ltd.
32 Lincoln Road
Olton
Birmingham, B27 6PA, UK.

ISBN 978-1-847194-10-7

www.packtpub.com

Cover Image by Vinayak Chittar (vinayak.chittar@gmail.com)

Credits

Author

Ramanujam Rao

Reviewers

Prabhat Jha

Russ Olsen

Senior Acquisition Editor

Rashmi Phadnis

Development Editor

Dhiraj Chandiramani

Technical Editor

Aanchal Kumar

Copy Editor

Sumathi Sridhar

Editorial Team Leader

Akshara Aware

Production Editorial Manager

Abhijeet Deobhakta

Project Team Leader

Lata Basantani

Project Coordinator

Leena Purkait

Indexer

Monica Ajmera

Proofreader

Dirk Manuel

Production Coordinator

Shantanu Zagade

Cover Work

Shantanu Zagade

About the Author

Ramanujam Rao is a software engineer, architect, and trainer specializing in building large-scale enterprise applications. He has over 13 years of experience in designing and developing complex web architectures, including portals, and helps enterprises in building scalable, distributed applications on the JEE platform.

He writes frequently on enterprise architecture, and actively consults in the field of information technology management, including technology platforms, technology strategy, and application delivery.

He has a B.S. in Electrical Engineering, an M.S. in Computer Science, and an MBA from Ohio State University. He currently lives and works in Columbus, OH, USA.

I'd like to thank my wife, Bharathi, and my daughter Gitanjali, for their constant support and for managing things during my long absences in the course of writing this book. I'd also like to acknowledge our parents, whose sacrifices and encouragement have always been part of everything I do.

I'd like to acknowledge the technology community in general, whose shoulders I stand on, including the folks at JBoss portal, and my colleagues at Nationwide Insurance.

Finally, a big thanks goes to the technical reviewers Russ and Prabhat, whose feedback was invaluable, and the entire Packt editorial team for their dilligence in getting the book out in a great shape.

About the Reviewers

Prabhat Jha works as Senior Engineer at JBoss, a division of Red Hat Inc. He has been working on JBoss Portal for the past two years, primarily on its integration aspects, performance, and scalability. He is also a contributor to PortletSwap (`http://www.jboss.org/portletswap`). He holds a Masters degree in Mathematics from the University of Texas in Austin, and has been working with Java and JEE for the past five years. He evangelizes portal technology at different Java User Groups (JUG).

Russ Olsen has been writing programs for over 25 years. During that time Russ has built systems in such diverse areas as low-level hardware control, inventory management and GIS, using everything from assembly language to Ruby. Active in both the Java and Ruby communities, Russ is the author of *Design Patterns In Ruby*.

Dedicated to my parents,
Narsingh and Bharathi Rao

Table of Contents

Preface

Enterprises need more than just basic services; they need value-creating entities, which are crucial for running a successful business. Portals offer tremendous value to enterprises, and JBoss Portal Server is a popular, feature-rich open-source server that provides a standards-compliant platform for hosting functionality that serves the diverse portal needs of an enterprise. Its primary strength lies in its ability to provide robust support for custom implementation of functionality using the JSR-168 portlet API.

This book is a practical guide to installing, configuring, and using JBoss Portal Server. It explains, with examples, how to easily build feature-rich portals using JBoss. As you move further on, you will learn to personalize your portals and add new features to them. This book will equip you with everything you need to know about JBoss Portal Server to build a fully-functional portal. It will help you to quickly understand and build enterprise portals with rich features, such as personalization, AJAX, single sign-on, Google widget integration, remote portlet integration, content management, and more. Along with feature implementation, the book will also provide developers with enough detail to be able to tune and customize the portal environment to best suit the platform needs.

What this book covers

Chapter 1 reviews portals, their functions, and their values. It talks about portal servers and the specifications that govern the creation and management of portals on the J2EE platform. Portal servers go beyond serving custom content and provide a feature-rich set of robust pre-built functions that take away the need to create certain fundamental sets of features from scratch each time. This chapter shows that, by removing the development efforts behind creating such features, portal developers can now spend their time and money on developing business functions.

Chapter 2 talks in detail about the installation process of JBoss portal, with an emphasis on the differences and caveats for the various installation types offered, depending on the usage scenarios. A simplified installation and deployment process facilitates faster implementation and fewer problems, as demonstrated by almost immediate creation and management of pages on the platform.

Chapter 3 goes a bit deeper into JBoss portal server and explains portlets better by creating a simple portlet application. It goes through the complete life cycle from code creation to deployment. This overview tour gives you a good idea of the major components that are required to create a functional portlet.

Chapter 4 reviews the various options that are available to effectively manage the presentation of portlets using technologies such as JSP, JSF, and so on. It shows a few examples of each one of them. To understand the concepts better, a portal application is created from scratch and a custom portlet, created with JSP-based view is added to this new application.

Chapter 5 reviews how the power of portals can be extended by facilitating features such as customization and personalization. It further extendeds our example portal to include custom layouts, themes, and other personalization features. It also shows how we can personalize a page and offer the users options for controlling the contents on the page.

Chapter 6 shows how JBoss portal blends the dynamism and rich functionality offered by AJAX with its strong portal architecture, to provide users with choices for developing highly-functional portal applications. It also discusses the limitations of the current specification and walks through an example that shows how easy it is to develop and deploy AJAX-based portlets.

Chapter 7 talks about how Hibernate, a very popular ORM tool, is used internally by JBoss applications, and how applications can integrate database support into portlet applications by using Hibernate.

Chapter 8 elaborates upon a simple but robust content management system provided by the JBoss portal that is sufficient for most of the needs for a portal application. Using interceptors, CMSAdmin, and CMS Portlets, the user can develop a functionality that helps to effectively manage and deliver content. This chapter extends our example further, to add some new content, and then edit it. It also shows how easy it is to add, edit, and manage content in the portal.

Chapter 9 discusses the various aspects of security as they relate to JBoss portal server and its functional components—the portal objects. JBoss portal allows a fine-grained level of control over portal objects such as portal instances, pages, and portlets. Security is an important function of an application. JBoss portal offers a varied set of options that allow the building of highly secure enterprise applications on the portal server.

Chapter 10 discusses the basics of remoting portlets before it goes into a few implementations using some real-world examples. It talks about how easily the portlets can be exposed as remotely available services, and how remote services can be consumed relatively effortlessly.

Chapter 11 talks about some of the features specified by the new portlet specification, such as portlet co-ordination, and filters introduction. It tells us how Portlet 2.0 provides a comprehensive set of options for performing robust portlet coordination by using events, as well as public parameters that tremendously increases the capabilities of portals and portlets by opening up possibilities for integrating not only within the application, but also with other applications within the enterprise.

Who this book is for

This book is for portal developers, administrators, designers and architects working on the Java platform, who want to build web portal solutions. The book doesn't expect an expert knowledge of portal or JEE technologies, but does presume a basic understanding of web technologies and the Java/JEE platform. However, the concepts are lucid enough that any competent developer can easily find immediate value in the book, and start creating dynamic portals.

Conventions

In this book, you will find a number of styles of text that distinguish between different kinds of information. Here are some examples of these styles, and an explanation of their meaning.

Code words in text are shown as follows: "We can include other contexts through the use of the `include` directive."

A block of code will be set as follows:

```
<web-app>
    <context-param>
        <param-name>
            org.jboss.jbossfaces.WAR_BUNDLES_JSF_IMPL
        </param-name>
        <param-value>true</param-value>
    </context-param>
</web-app>
```

When we wish to draw your attention to a particular part of a code block, the relevant lines or items will be set in bold:

```
<script type="text/javascript"></script>
<!-- inject the theme, default to the Renewal theme if nothing is
  selected for the portal or the page -->
<p:theme themeName="renewal"/>
<!-- insert header content that was possibly set by portlets on
  the page -->
<p:headerContent/>
```

New terms and **important words** are introduced in a bold-type font. Words that you see on the screen, in menus or dialog boxes for example, appear in our text like this: "Clicking on the **Configure Dashboard** link will take us to the page which provides interface to design our dashboard".

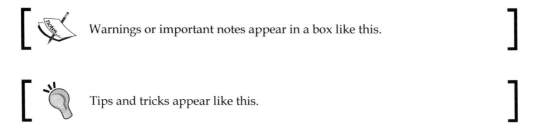

Warnings or important notes appear in a box like this.

Tips and tricks appear like this.

Reader feedback

Feedback from our readers is always welcome. Let us know what you think about this book—what you liked or may have disliked. Reader feedback is important for us to develop titles that you really get the most out of.

To send us general feedback, simply send an email to feedback@packtpub.com, making sure that you mention the book title in the subject of your message.

If there is a book that you need and would like to see us publish, please send us a note via the **SUGGEST A TITLE** form on www.packtpub.com, or send an email to suggest@packtpub.com.

If there is a topic that you have expertise in and you are interested in either writing or contributing to a book on, see our author guide on www.packtpub.com/authors.

Customer support

Now that you are the proud owner of a Packt book, we have a number of things to help you to get the most from your purchase.

Downloading the example code for the book

Visit http://www.packtpub.com/files/code/4107_Code.zip to download the example code.

The downloadable files contain instructions on how to use them.

Errata

Although we have taken every care to ensure the accuracy of our contents, mistakes do happen. If you find a mistake in one of our books—maybe a mistake in text or code—we would be grateful if you would report this to us. By doing so you can save other readers from frustration, and help to improve subsequent versions of this book. If you find any errata, report them by visiting http://www.packtpub.com/support, selecting your book, clicking on the **let us know** link, and entering the details of your errata. Once your errata are verified, your submission will be accepted and the errata added to any list of existing errata. Existing errata can be viewed by selecting your title from http://www.packtpub.com/support.

Piracy

Piracy of copyright material on the Internet is an ongoing problem across all media. At Packt, we take the protection of our copyright and licenses very seriously. If you come across any illegal copies of our works in any form on the Internet, please provide the location address or website name immediately so we can pursue a remedy.

Please contact us at copyright@packtpub.com with a link to the suspected pirated material.

We appreciate your help in protecting our authors, and our ability to bring you valuable content.

Questions

You can contact us at `questions@packtpub.com` if you are having a problem with some aspect of the book, and we will do our best to address it.

1
Portals and Portal Servers

A portal in the true sense of the word, is a common entrance to a destination. Portals on the Internet, also called web portals, are a single entry point to an application that provides varied features such as personalized and aggregated content, search capabilities, and customized applications.

Portals have gained significant popularity as a means for generating business values through efficient marketing, sales, and services, as well as being a channel for providing timely, useful, and accurate information and services to users.

In this chapter, we will review the basics of web portals, their types, differentiating characteristics, and uses.

Later in the chapter, we will also talk about portal servers, their types, applications architecture, and governing specifications. Portlets are independent pieces of functions that constitute a portal application. We will also briefly discuss how these basic building blocks help in providing the overall value for a portal application.

Portals

Today, information from web sites is not only served through static web sites, but also through focused and customized gateways targeted at a specific customer segment. Towards that goal, portals have gained significant popularity in the past few years as an efficient, convenient, and effective way of organizing, aggregating, and customizing information for users. Portals are particularly effective in enterprises, where the challenges of information management and delivery are overwhelming. They can offer an approach to leveraging existing IT investments and seamlessly integrating diverse functionality through a single, user-friendly channel.

Broadly, the features offered by portals are as follows:

- **Content Management and Aggregation**: Content can be effectively and efficiently managed to provide a single consistent view of the enterprise to a user. Disparate enterprise applications serving information through multiple outlets can be aggregated into a single channel.

- **Personalization and Customization**: When content is aggregated and users are served through a single channel, personalizing and customizing the content provides added usability. Storing and remembering preferences gives an incentive for users to build a portal that best serves their time and interests.

- **Search**: A portal, being the entrance to all applications and content, is almost expected to provide search functionality. Portals have varying levels of integration with search functionality across content in the enterprise. Portals can either come with limited search capabilities built into them, or they can provide easy hooks to other standalone search engines that are already available in the enterprise.

- **Seamless Authentication**: Authentication, single sign-on, and authorization are various techniques to control access to applications. When users access applications independently, they are required to provide credentials separately for each application. When a portal integrates all these applications, it also provides an easy way to manage credentials beyond a single application, seamlessly allowing access to other enterprise applications without logging in again. This results in better usability and decreased exposure to security threats.

- **Collaboration**: This is a feature that has gained popularity in the recent years. A single platform for all enterprise applications usually results in better collaboration among various application owners. However, with growing interest in social networking and collaborative efforts, portals are now increasingly offering added features as a part of their value-added set. Having all of the users residing on a single platform provides a great opportunity for the portal to facilitate easy information exchange and collaboration between the users.

Why portals?

Portals have gained acceptance in the enterprise due to their capability to streamline and organize diverse applications through a single channel. The productivity gains experienced by an employee, customer, or a partner clearly provide immense functional value to an enterprise, due to features such as easy access to a wide array of enterprise resources, consolidated search capability and content management. Similarly, enhanced user experience through customized content, persistent preferences, and single/seamless sign-on access result in satisfied users.

Due to the need to consolidate applications and content across the enterprise, portals provide subsidiary benefits of aligning business units in terms of the applications they create and the content they generate, with a single customer/user view.

Some of the benefits of having portals are listed here:

- Real-time management of consistent and trusted content along with timely publication, using a well controlled workflow.
- Efficient business processes with effective synergies.
- A single channel view of enterprise data and content through aggregated search capabilities.
- Enhanced communications between users and the enterprise through timely and relevant publication of information and use of a collaboration toolset. Employees, partners, and customers can now depend on a single channel to get a view of the enterprise and its functions, instead of having to refer to multiple outlets.
- Significant user retention and continued use of the channel due to strong personalization and usability features.
- Lower the total cost of ownership, by using open source software and increase the return on investments through improved visibility, productivity, and process efficiency.

Types of portals

Portals can be categorized in many ways. However, the most logical way of classifying them is based on the functionality they provide, and the users they cater to. Function-based categorization focuses on the former, while user-based categorization focuses on the latter.

Function-based portals

Based on the functionality offered by portals, they can be classified as vertical portals or horizontal portals. These include both portals offered within the enterprise and portals that provide standalone applications on the Internet.

Vertical portal

Vertical portals, also called **Vortals** are the types of portals that are built to provide a full-stack implementation of single business functionality. All of the sub-elements of a vertical portal are built to provide different features of a single business function. Vertical portals are very popular among electronic and web-based business web sites.

Web-based business application users prefer a feature-rich application with easy access to functionality and a productive user experience. Vertical portals try to provide all possible features to a user in the most efficient way, centered around the business function, thus making the experience of doing business mutually valuable to both the users and the business.

Web sites offered by brokerage houses, medical/health services, and so on, are almost always vertical portals, where their customers are provided with various services related to their businesses. As seen in the following example, the business uses a vertical portal to provide all the services related to its business to the user through a single channel. The various page segments are independent functionalities, but they all are a part of the offerings of the same business function.

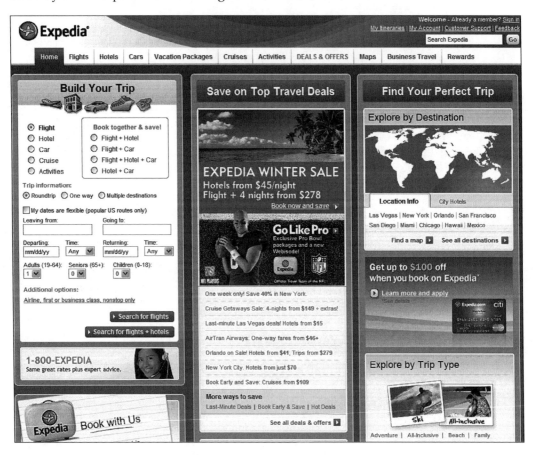

Horizontal portal

Horizontal portals offer a broad set of functions that are not aligned to a single scope, function, or capability. The idea here is to provide users with a set of aggregated information from various disparate sources based on some loosely defined categories. Each individual portal segment is unrelated to the other, and each operates independently in terms of content, scope, and function. Horizontal portals are typically built to cater to a broader audience that has diverse interests and preferences. This is different from vertical portals, which are built for a specific audience with a focused scope.

Web sites such as iGoogle, Yahoo!, and so on, are prime examples of horizontal portals. As seen in the following screenshot, the horizontal portal provides functions from various unrelated sources, but together, they meet the diverse needs of the user.

User-based portals

User-based classification is a different way of looking at portals, and here, portals are categorized based on the type of users who use the portal. These users can be other businesses, customers, or employees. Hence, we have new sub-categories such as **B2B (Business to Business)**, **B2C (Business to Consumer)**, and **B2E (Business to Employee)**.

B2B portal

This type of portal is built for interaction with other businesses, as opposed to direct customers. A B2B portal facilitates activities between businesses that are a part of their business workflow. Examples of these are verifications, transactions, approvals, reports, and so on, all without manual intervention. Some good examples are companies that offer EDI services to others businesses, who then retrieve the data as and when required. Logistics management in businesses leverages such B2B services for activities such as order processing, fulfillment, and so on. B2B portals are usually used by businesses as a method of servicing their customers, and are less reliant on personalization and user interface aspects, when compared to other portal types.

With the increasing popularity of the Internet-based transactions, improved reliability, higher bandwidth, and so on, more and more businesses are, today, looking at reducing construction costs and expanding B2B portals to serve their business customers, who in turn, are constantly looking for ways to optimize their processes through automation.

B2C portal

These are the most common type of portals, and encompass pretty much all e-commerce web sites that deal with customers directly. Examples of these portals are amazon.com, walmart.com, and so on. Instead of software systems and businesses interacting with the portal, a B2C directly interacts with the end customers, and hence, personalization, user interface, and user experience are of significant importance if the business wants to attract and retain its customers.

B2E portal

This type of portal can also be termed as an intranet portal; a B2E portal is built by a company or a business as a source of information and services for the exclusive use of internal company employees. Unlike a corporate intranet static web site, which is very generic in terms of its content and audience, a B2E portal is built to offer tailored information to an employee depending, typically, on his or her position, role, and location in the organization. Examples of the information and services provided by a B2E portal are: vacation reporting, performance summary, time management, resource ordering, pay information, and any specific — possibly sensitive — notifications.

Portal servers

Portal servers are software implementations of portal functionalities. They come either as standalone applications, tightly integrated with the application server they are built on, or they come as separate applications that can be deployed on an application server of choice. In this book, we will use the word portal to indicate a portal server.

A typical enterprise portal architecture is depicted in the following figure:

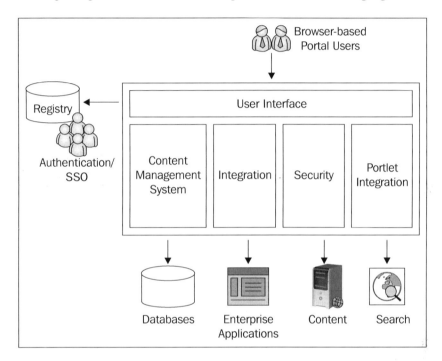

Fundamentally, today's enterprise portals can be viewed as aggregators of structured and unstructured data, which provide a consistent view to the end user. In our case, the structured data is represented by the RDBMS, and the unstructured data is depicted as XML or RSS feeds. Apart from data, portals also integrate with enterprise services.

As seen in the previous figure, the major components of a modern portal architecture are as follows:

- **User Interface**: This is the interaction layer with the client and is responsible for handling HTTP requests, generating appropriate responses, and aggregating content to create a single page.

- **Portlet Integration**: Portlets are pluggable, independently deployable, and executable pieces of functionality that help constitute a web page served from a portal. This is the core of the services provided by a portal and plays the important function of managing the life cycle and behavior of the portlets.

- **Content Management and Publishing**: This component is responsible for providing functionality to edit content, manage workflow, and schedule publication. The content is provided from repositories either internal or external to the portal. External content also includes data feeds.

- **Security**: Integrated components provide authentication and single sign-on features using enterprise registries.

- **Integration Interfaces**: These interfaces facilitate easy integration with other external resources, services, and applications. Given that a part of a portal's role is aggregation of various enterprise systems, having strong integration features with support for components and protocols adds a definite value.

Portals provide their differentiating functions by leveraging their core components and integrating with other external entities, such as databases, services, search engines, and enterprise applications. There are many popular portal server implementations in the industry today, providing a diverse set of features and implementing specifications to varying degrees. Examples of these are **IBM Websphere Portal Server**, **BEA Portal**, **LifeRay**, and **JBoss Portal Server**.

Portlets and portlet container

Portals are implemented in various technologies. In this book, we will focus on J2EE technology and portal implementation on that platform.

As with any other API or feature in J2EE, portal and portal server implementations are governed by commonly-agreed industry standards and specifications. JSR-168 and JSR-286, also called the Portlet Specifications, govern the standards for portal technology on the J2EE platform. Before we go further into the portal server architecture, let us review some terminology.

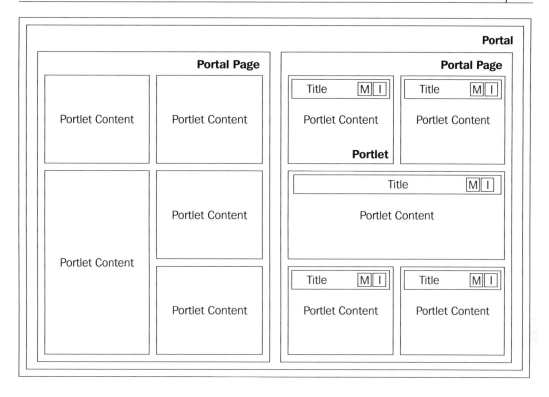

The components of this figure are described here:

- **Portal**: This is a web application that runs on an application server, hosts the presentation layer, and provides foundational services such as single sign-on, personalization, content aggregation, and so on.

- **Portlet**: A portlet is Java-based, built to specification, independent, and a self-contained piece of functionality that contributes to a portal page and leverages the foundational functionality provided by the portal. A portlet generates its relevant page fragment that, along with other portlets, constitutes the user interface of a portal page. A browser interacts with each portlet through the portal, where the requests are processed by the portlet before returning the response again through the portal.

- **Portal Page**: This is a web page that aggregates portlets into a single HTML page, which the portlet container compiles and sends back to the browser client.

- **Portlet Container**: A portlet container manages the life cycle of portlets and provides them with the appropriate runtime environment. The container stores the preferences for each portlet and works with the portal to ensure effective request/response communication to and from portlets. It only deals with the portals' behavior and their mutual communication. Aspects such as content aggregation are delegated to the higher portal.

Constructing a view

Let us look at an example of how these components are used. The following figure shows a high-level view of how a portal processes a request, and the specific role of the components of the portal:

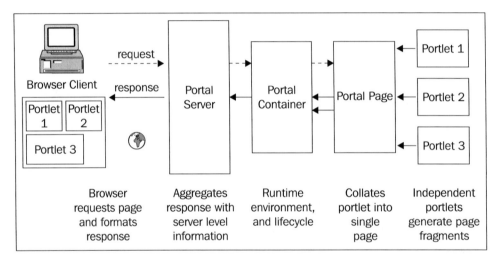

As we can see, the browser makes the request for a portal page, which is then passed to the portal container by the server that had originally received the request. The container determines the appropriate page and passes the request to it. The portal page identifies all the portlets contributing to it, and aggregates all the page fragments generated by each portlet. Each portlet independently follows its own life cycle and generates the final fragment. The combined page is then passed back to the container, which then passes the response back to the server. The server aggregates the information along with its own features, and returns the response to the browser, which formats the HTML for the user.

Portal specification and WSRP

JSR-168 and **JSR-286** are **Java Portlet Specifications** that define the standard for the Java Portlet API. Like other specifications, the portlet API specification is intended for both portlet developers and portal server creators. Standardizing on a portlet API allows the creation of pluggable portlets that are independent of the portal server. Hence, the portlets created on one platform can be easily migrated to another.

The Web Services for Remote Portlets (WSRP) specification defines a protocol for creating and communicating with remote portlets. It is not intended to compete with the portlet specifications; instead, it facilitates web services based communication between portlets created using the specification. Because application integration is the primary function of portals, utilizing web services for integration can be an efficient mechanism.

Servlets and portlets

J2EE Servlets and Portlets share a lot of features. Both are Java-based web components, whose life cycles are managed by the container, interacting with browser clients, servicing requests, and responding to them. Both are also responsible for generating dynamic content to create the user interface of the web application. However, portlets differ from servlets in terms of scope and functionality in the following ways:

- Portlets are not accessible by a URL. Portlets are intended to be part of a page, as opposed to being independent pages.

- Browsers and web clients interact with portlets through the portal server. Portlets can neither set HTTP headers, nor be aware of the client URL.

- The portal server provides a customized subset of the request object to a portlet.

- Portlets only contribute a fragment of the HTML page that is eventually presented to the browser, and not the whole page. A portal server aggregates these fragments from various portlets to create a final page.

- Portlets come with certain modes and window states that make them function independently of the whole page behavior.

- Portlets have access to some specialized functionality that allows storage of states and preferences across requests and sessions.

The expectations from portals are different from traditional web sites. Hence, the portlet specifications have to be created independently of servlets.

However, this doesn't preclude portals from interacting with servlets. A portlet can effectively invoke any servlet, JSP, or a JSP tag, and leverage their functionality to fulfill its function.

Summary

In enterprises today, portals provide a wide variety of services not just to their employees, but also to their customers and business partners. In this chapter, we have reviewed portals, their functions, and their values. Today, portals have moved beyond providing basic servicing functions to customers, to becoming differentiating and value-creating entities, crucial for running a successful business.

We also talked about portal servers and specifications governing the creation and management of portals on the J2EE platform. Portal servers go beyond serving custom content and provide a default and feature-rich set of robust pre-built functions that take away the need for creating certain fundamental sets of features from scratch each time. By removing the development efforts behind creating such features, portal developers can now spend their time and money on developing business functions. In the coming chapters, we will dig deeper into portal implementations using one of the popular open source portal servers—the JBoss portal server.

2
Getting Started with JBoss Portal

JBoss portal server is one of the popular and feature-rich open source servers that provide a standards-compliant platform to host functionality that serves the diverse portal needs of an enterprise.

In this chapter, we will briefly get acquainted with JBoss Portal, review its features, and find out why it is one of the better portal software applications in the industry. We will also get into the details of downloading and installing the server and will later look at putting things into action by creating and customizing a page that demonstrates the features of the portal.

JBoss portal server

JBoss portal server is a leading provider of an open source portal framework, enriched with content management functionality. It provides a robust and rich features set, compliant with the industry standards JSR-168 and JSR-286. These specifications facilitate a pluggable architecture for modules, including security and workflow, WSRP, and so on, for easy integration with the platform. JBoss portal server is provided under the business-friendly LGPL license, and optimized to run on the widely popular open source JBoss Application Server.

There are other portal framework providers in the industry today that offer a standards compliant features-set, but JBoss provides value through a zero-cost, feature-rich, quality portal server combined with a robust and scalable underlying application server platform.

Features

The features that JBoss portal server provides are a combination of its compliance with the specification, the support of the underlying JBoss application server, and its own value-add set.

The following categorization is only to list the salient features of the software as of version 2.7.0, the version used throughout the book. A detailed list can be found on the JBoss portal web site at `http://www.jboss.com/products/platforms/portals`.

Technology and Architecture

- **Standards-based implementation**: Platform compliant to the JSR-168, JSR-286, and Portlet 2.0 specification
- **JEMS**: Leverages the power of **JBoss Enterprise Middleware Services**—JBoss application server, JBoss cache, JGroups, and Hibernate
- **Scalability**: Provides support for clustering portal states for all instances

Security and Single Sign On

- Out-of-the-box support for **SSO** and, integration with JOSSO and CAS
- **JAAS Authentication**: Custom authentication via JAAS login modules
- **LDAP Integration**: Easy integration with LDAP servers
- **User Management**: Easy user registration, management and access controls

Supported Standards

- Portlet Specification (JSR-168, JSR-286)
- Java Server Faces 1.2, 2.0 (JSR-252, JSR-314)
- Web Services for Remote Portlets (WSRP) 1.0
- J2EE 1.4 with JBoss Application Server

Portal and Portlet Container

- **Multiple Portal Instances**: Ability to have multiple portal instances running inside one portal container
- **Inter-Portlet Communication (IPC) API**: Allows portlets to create links to other objects such as a page, portal, or window
- **Application Development Framework Support**: Struts, Spring MVC, and MyFaces

- **Internationalization**: Ability to use internationalization features at a granular level
- **Page-based Architecture**: Allows grouping of portlets on a per-page basis

Content Management System

- **Full Directory and File Support**: Creates, moves, deletes, copies, and uploads entire directory trees or files
- **Full-featured WYSIWYG HTML editor**: HTML Editor contains WYSIWYG mode, preview functionality, and HTML source editing mode
- **Versioning support**: All content, either edited or created, is auto-versioned with a viewable history
- **Internationalization Support**: Content can be attributed to a specific locale and then served to the user based on his or her browser settings
- **Basic Workflow Support**: Submission for review and approval process

Installing the server

Now that we are aware, and presumably excited about the features JBoss portal server offers, let's get started with downloading and installing it.

The following sections provide an overview of the installation process, which should be sufficient for most installs. However, for complicated scenarios or for more in-depth information, it might be a good idea to also refer to the advanced documentation provided by JBoss at `http://www.jboss.org/jbossportal/docs/index.html`.

Getting the software

Just like any other open source software, getting the JBoss portal server software is as simple as going to the JBoss web site and downloading it.

The web site offers different versions of software for different installation scenarios. Options include a version packaged along with JBoss application server platform, an independent binary for installs on existing servers or clustered environments, and a version in source code format that a user can use to build a binary. This allows us to choose from a wide array of options ranging from, standalone portal servers and pre-packaged version with application servers, to building from source.

System requirements

Before we go into the details of installation, let's quickly review the minimum system requirements to run JBoss Portal Server 2.7.0

- **JBoss Application Server (AS) 4.2.3, JBoss Enterprise Application Platform (EAP) 4.2**, and **JBoss EAP 4.3**. In addition to the JBoss application server, the portal is designed to work on application servers such as **Weblogic** and **Websphere**. However, it is recommended that JBoss servers are used, for maximum value.

- The portal, being a 100 percent pure Java application, is independent of the underlying platform. Thus, JBoss portal server can be successfully deployed and run on any platform that supports a **Java Virtual Machine (JVM)**.

- JDK5

- 512 MB RAM

- Approximately 100MB hard disk space

- A minimum 400MHz CPU

- JBoss portal uses **Hibernate** to implement persistence. Hibernate provides extensive support for all the popular databases, hence making the portal server compatible with most databases.

Installation

The server can be installed in different ways depending on the type of software downloaded. The three versions are:

1. JBoss portal and JBoss AS bundle
2. JBoss portal server binary
3. JBoss portal source

In the next few sections, we will discuss the server installation for each of these versions. The complexity of the installation ranges from a simple installation of the bundled software version to complex source compilation and independent installation on an existing application server.

JBoss portal packaged with JBoss application server

This is probably the easiest installation method, and is recommended for anybody who is a beginner with JBoss portal, or wishes to install and explore the product. This version includes JBoss portal server and the underlying JBoss application server. The server comes with default set of configuration options along with a inbuilt Hypersonic SQL database.

We need to execute the following steps to install JBoss portal and JBoss application server bundle:

1. After downloading the ZIP file containing the bundled software, extract the ZIP file into a convenient directory. Please note that in this installation method, the directory chosen is permanent and will be used for every JBoss portal artifact. In other words, there won't be any installation files or software binaries outside this directory, making it a very clean and convenient install. A typical directory on Windows is c:\jboss-portal-2.7.0.

   After expanding the ZIP file, the structure looks like this:

   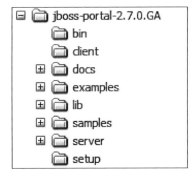

2. Run the executable in the JBOSS_PORTAL_INSTALLATION/bin/ directory. The executables are run.bat for a Windows installation, or run.sh for UNIX systems. During startup, the server uses a default configuration. However, if we want to provide an alternate configuration file, we need to use the -c option along with run.bat or run.sh.

3. Point your browser to the URL `http://localhost:8080/portal`, and you should see the default portal home page as shown in the following screenshot. The portal provides two accounts by default for user log-in. The login parameters for the first account are username *user* and password *user*, and for the second account are username *admin* and password: *admin*. Each of the IDs has special relevance and access rights associated with it. We will come back to this topic later when we talk about portal security, for now it is sufficient to use these IDs as listed.

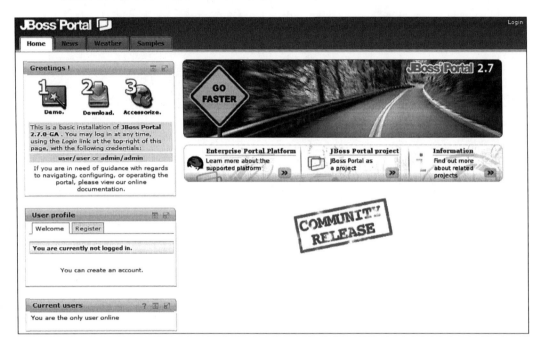

During the execution of the `run` script, the console will show a few errors and warnings, as shown in the following screenshot. The reason is, during start-up, JBoss Portal looks for certain initial database tables and if it doesn't find them, it creates them, with a warning message. Given that this is the first time, it cannot find them. It is okay to ignore these errors and warnings.

```
18:36:16,095 ERROR [JDBCExceptionReporter] Table not found in statement [select
top ? persistent0_.PK as PK81_, persistent0_.HANDLE as HANDLE81_, persistent0_.S
TATUS as STATUS81_, persistent0_.CONSUMER_PK as CONSUMER4_81_ from JBP_PORTLET_R
EG persistent0_]
18:36:16,095 WARN  [JDBCExceptionReporter] SQL Error: -22, SQLState: S0002
18:36:16,095 ERROR [JDBCExceptionReporter] Table not found in statement [select
top ? persistent0_.PK as PK76_, persistent0_.PORTLET_ID as PORTLET2_76_, persist
ent0_.REGISTRATION_ID as REGISTRA3_76_, persistent0_.REGISTRATION_TIME as REGIST
RA4_76_, persistent0_.TERMINATION_TIME as TERMINAT5_76_, persistent0_.PARENT_PK
as PARENT6_76_ from JBP_PORTLET_STATE persistent0_]
18:36:16,105 WARN  [JDBCExceptionReporter] SQL Error: -22, SQLState: S0002
18:36:16,105 ERROR [JDBCExceptionReporter] Table not found in statement [select
top ? persistent0_.PK as PK77_, persistent0_.NAME as NAME77_, persistent0_.TYPE
as TYPE77_, persistent0_.READ_ONLY as READ4_77_ from JBP_PORTLET_STATE_ENTRY per
sistent0_]
18:36:16,105 WARN  [JDBCExceptionReporter] SQL Error: -22, SQLState: S0002
18:36:16,105 ERROR [JDBCExceptionReporter] Table not found in statement [select
top ? persistent0_.PK as PK79_, persistent0_.ID as ID79_, persistent0_.STATUS as
STATUS79_ from JBP_PORTLET_GROUP persistent0_]
```

Sometimes, during startup, the server might give an
OutOfMemoryError. This can be eliminated by adjusting the
MaxPermSize in the startup options. Just add
-XX:MaxPermSize=128M to JAVA_OPTS in the run script.

JBoss portal binary without the server

This installation method is recommended if you want to install only the portal binary
and already have a pre-existing installation of JBoss AS or JBoss EAP on which the
portal will run. This method is also used when you want to install JBoss portal in a
clustered environment.

The following steps should be followed to install JBoss portal binary:

1. Download and extract the ZIP archive in a temporary directory. After some
   configuration, we will move segments of the content to the permanent,
   application server tree.

   The binary version can be found on the same download page as was listed
   under the section *JBoss Portal Binary*.

   Once extracted, the structure looks like this:

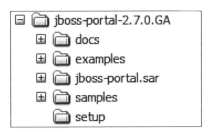

The significant difference here is that the downloadable now consists primarily of a service archive, or a `sar` directory called `jboss-portal.sar`. This is where the portal software and configurations reside. It also has a `setup` directory, which has datasource descriptors and configurations for various databases, so that the portal can connect to the databases on the existing server platform.

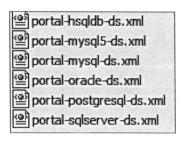

portal-hsqldb-ds.xml
portal-mysql5-ds.xml
portal-mysql-ds.xml
portal-oracle-ds.xml
portal-postgresql-ds.xml
portal-sqlserver-ds.xml

2. Configure the JBoss application server or JBoss EAP. For our current purpose, it is assumed that either the JBoss application server or JBoss EAP has already been installed and configured. For more detailed documentation on the installation of these servers, please refer to the specific documentation provided by JBoss.

3. Configure the database and datasources.

As mentioned earlier, the binary install option is best suited for an existing application server. Hence, the likely scenario for its use will be in a non-development environment. JBoss portal requires a database to be run. Even though JBoss application server comes with in-built support for the HypersonicSQL database, it is recommended that the portal server does not use this database beyond development. It is recommended that a separate RDBMS be installed, and the portal configured to use it.

Before we begin the configuration of the portal server, let's look at the installation and configuration of the external database, and briefly touch upon the parts that are relevant to the portal install.

To use a database with the portal, the following are the salient steps:

  i.   Create a new database instance and name it, for example, `jbportal`.

  ii. Grant access rights to a user on the portal that will actively use the database `jbportal`. The portal uses the user to create tables and modify data in the tables in the database. Hence, it will require the rights to do so. This same user will be used when we configure the database descriptor in the portal configuration.

iii. To connect an RDBMS database, J2EE application server leverage connectors, also called JDBC drivers, are provided by the database vendors. Drivers help connect applications, such as portals deployed on application servers, to RDBMS databases. The drivers can be found on the web sites of the database vendors. The JDBC driver `jarfile` is copied to the sever directory at `$JBOSS_HOME/server/default/lib/`, where `$JBOSS_HOME` is the home directory of the server installation.

iv. To configure the datasources in the portal server, we will edit the XML descriptor file corresponding to our database in the `setup` directory under the extracted portal tree discussed in Step 1.

Let's assume that our database is MySQL v5, so the descriptor we will edit is `portal-mysql5-ds.xml`.

The file, edited with appropriate values, will appear as follows. Please refer to the documentation provided by the database vendor for advanced configuration options in the connection URL.

```xml
<?xml version="1.0" encoding="UTF-8"?>
<datasources>
  <local-tx-datasource>
    <jndi-name>PortalDS</jndi-name>
    <connection-url>jdbc:mysql://localhost:3306/jbportal</connection-url>
    <driver-class>com.mysql.jdbc.Driver</driver-class>
    <user-name>portal</user-name>
    <password>portalpassword</password>
  </local-tx-datasource>
</datasources>
```

4. Deploy the JBoss portal binary.

Once we are ready with the database and have configured our descriptor, we are ready to deploy the portal server software on the application server. The file `mysql5-ds.xml` is first copied to the `$JBOSS_HOME/server/configuration/deploy/` directory, where `configuration` is either `all`, `default`, `minimal`, or `production`, depending on the type and installation of the application server. This step will ensure that the server is aware of the new database, and is ready to offer connections, when requested by the portal. However, when we add a new datasource configuration, we have to make sure that we remove the default Hypersonic SQL Db configuration file from the directory, to avoid conflicts.

The whole subdirectory `jboss-portal.sar`, from the original downloaded binary as detailed in Step 1, is now copied to the `$JBOSS_HOME/server/con-figuration/deploy/` directory, where again the `configuration` value is set depending on the type and installation of the application server. With this, the application server is aware of the existence of the JBoss portal in a service archive format, which will automatically get deployed and started when the application server starts up.

5. As with the earlier install, we can now direct the browser to the URL `http://localhost:8080/portal`, and we should see the default portal home page. The userid/password options, as before, are **user/user** and **admin/admin**.

    During the start-up process, we should see the errors and warnings related to missing tables, as detailed in the bundled version section. Again, these can be ignored as they are simply the portal's first-time execution symptoms.

Building JBoss portal from source

As with all open source software, JBoss portal can also be downloaded in source form and built to create a deployable artifact. Needless to say, this option is recommended only for experts and individuals who are comfortable dealing with raw source code and the complexities associated with building from source.

We will not go into a lot of detail for this installation method, as the options are broad and subject to various preferences of the user. Exhaustive and specific information on building from sources can be found on the JBoss forums and in the associated documentation.

Configuration

Once the server is installed, we can plan on customizing it to our environment and setting up the values that will facilitate effective functioning of the server.

There are several configuration parameters that can be configured or changed in the server, such as context root, email, ports, and so on. In this section, we will talk about a few important ones.

Changing the context root

The default context path for the portal is /portal, and the portal server responds on http://localhost:8080/portal. However, the context path can be changed to a path of your choice by editing the web server configuration file in both the bundled version as well as the binary sar versions. For source builds, the change needs to go into a property file before the server is built.

To change the context path in the configuration file, we will need to edit the file $JBOSS_HOME/server/default/deploy/jboss-portal.sar/portal-server.war/WEB-INF/jboss-web.xml

We then need to change the value of the element, <context-root> from portal to the desired value. As seen in the following screenshot, the value is changed from portal to archway:

```
<?xml version="1.0"?>
<jboss-web>
    <security-domain>java:jaas/portal</security-domain>
    <context-root>/archway</context-root>
    <replication-config>
        <replication-trigger>SET</replication-trigger>
    </replication-config>
    <resource-ref>
        <res-ref-name>jdbc/PortalDS</res-ref-name>
        <jndi-name>java:PortalDS</jndi-name>
    </resource-ref>
</jboss-web>
```

Once this file has been changed and saved and the server has been restarted, the portal server now responds on http://localhost:8080/archway.

Changing the portal port

To change the default port setting, we need to edit the $JBOSS_HOME/server/default/deploy/jboss-web.deployer/server.xml file. Under the jboss.web service node, we need to change the value of the element <Connector port=> to port 80.

The updated configuration is as follows:

```
<Service name="jboss.web">
 <Connector port="80" address="${jboss.bind.address}"
     maxThreads="250" maxHttpHeaderSize="8192"
     emptySessionPath="true" protocol="HTTP/1.1"
     enableLookups="false" redirectPort="8443" acceptCount="100"
     connectionTimeout="20000" disableUploadTimeout="true" />
```

It is important that when the port is changed, any dependencies such as remoting portlets or WSRP settings are also updated. We will talk about remote portlets in later sections of this chapter.

Setting email service

Emails are used for workflow processes, or to verify registered users. JBoss portal, by default, assumes an SMTP server on the local machine on which it runs. Sometimes, it is a good idea to set up email configuration during installation. To change the default setting, the `$JBOSS_HOME/server/default/deploy/jboss-portal.sar/META-INF/jboss-service.xml` file needs to be edited.

The MBean configuration for mail can be changed to point to a different mail gateway with appropriate authentication credentials.

The following figure shows an updated configuration using a remote SMTP server with a user ID and password.

```
<mbean
    code="org.jboss.portal.core.impl.mail.MailModuleImpl"
    name="portal:service=Module,type=Mail"
    xmbean-dd=""
    xmbean-code="org.jboss.portal.jems.as.system.JBossServiceModelMBean">
    <xmbean/>
    <depends>jboss:service=Mail</depends>
    <depends>portal:service=Module,type=IdentityServiceController</depends>
    <attribute name="QueueCapacity">-1</attribute>
    <attribute name="Gateway">smtp.aol.com</attribute>
    <attribute name="SmtpUser">test</attribute>
    <attribute name="SmtpPassword">test</attribute>
    <attribute name="JavaMailDebugEnabled">false</attribute>
    <attribute name="SMTPConnectionTimeout">100000</attribute>
    <attribute name="SMTPTimeout">10000</attribute>
    <attribute name="JNDIName">java:portal/MailModule</attribute>
</mbean>
```

Configuring proxies

Some of the portlets in the server, such as weather, stock tickers, and so on, require Internet access to request and present updated information. Similarly, to request and process RSS feeds, the server needs to access the Internet. Some enterprises do not have direct access to the Internet and require access through proxy servers.

The portal server can be configured to use proxies by adding the JAVA_OPTS environment variable to the portal server startup script when Java is invoked to start the JVM.

A typical setting option is as follows:

```
-Dhttp.proxyHost=proxy.xyz.net  -Dhttp.proxyPort=8118
```

Working with the portal

Now that we have installed and configured our portal server, it is time to dig in and start playing with it. The portal server can be interacted with in multiple ways. In this section, we will get started and introduce ourselves to the user interface offered by the portal, and the basics of interacting with the portal. We will also discuss some features that are offered, before finally testing the portal with our very own custom portal page with portlets.

Getting started

A portal server consists of several portals, each portal consists of portal pages, and each page consists of portlets.

As seen in the following screenshot of the portal home page depicted in the following screenshot, the default portal we have just installed consists of four portal pages, **Home**, **News**, **Weather**, and **Samples**:

The default portal page called **Home** consists of four portlets, namely, **Greetings**, **User Profile**, **Current Users** (on the left side), and **Content View** (on the right). The **Greetings**, **User Profile**, and **Current Users** portlets have simple and obvious functions, and their window states can be changed by interacting with the decoration buttons in the upper-right section of each portlet window. The content view on the right has no decorations, and hence has a default static behavior.

We can continue to explore the default portal pages as an anonymous user, or we can log in to the portal and customize the content for ourselves. To log in, we can register ourselves using the **User profile** portlet on the default home page. For now, we will use the default user ID and password that come with the JBoss portal installation.

After we enter the credentials by clicking on the **Login** link on the upper-right of the page, we reach the home page that is now owned by user *user*. The home page is a standard page set by the administrator for all users, but the dashboard is a customized version created by the user.

Using an administrator account provides a lot more features in terms of the content management of portal home pages, account management, and access control. We will discuss these in detail in the subsequent chapters of this book. For now, we will continue with our understanding of the portal server by creating simple pages for a regular user account.

Creating our first portal page

A portal page is basically an aggregation of portlets, with decorated windows and content. Let's try and create a portal page using the JBoss portal platform.

After we logged in as *user*, we can begin to personalize and customize the portal by updating existing pages and creating new ones. The link on the upper-right of the screen, called **Dashboard**, takes us to a dashboard with content personalized to suit our needs. At this time, there is only a single page titled **Home** for the user *user* with limited functionality. Let us customize our dashboard by adding another page.

Clicking on the **Configure Dashboard** link will take us to the page that provides us with an interface that we can use to design our dashboard. The personal dashboard editor page is shown in the following screenshot:

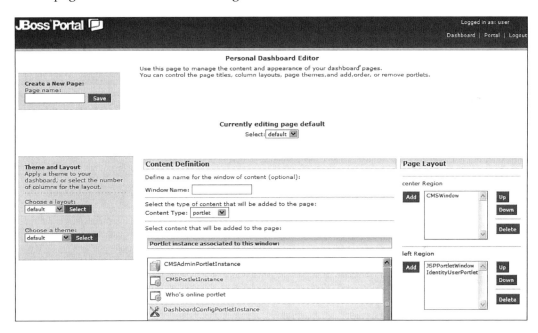

We can use this page to either edit existing pages or to create new ones. Let us create a new page called **First** by entering the name in the upper-left section of the page, which is titled **Create a New Page**.

The page is now selected for editing by default, and we are ready to design the page and add content to it. We will leave the **Theme and Layout** sections with their default values, and focus instead on the **Content Definition** and **Page Layout** sections.

We will start by adding content of the type *portlet*, and picking the **RSS portlet Yahoo finance** from the following list. We will then add this portlet to the leftmost region of the new page called **First**. The screen should then appear as shown in the following screenshot:

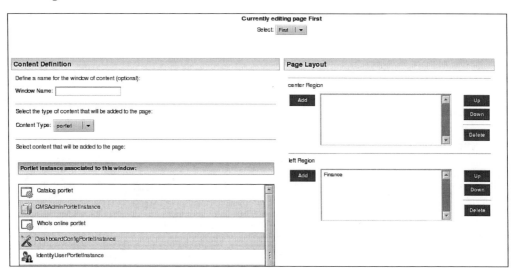

Now, let's add another content of type widget—Google. Google widgets are small pieces of functionality that can be embedded in pages. We will use the first widget titled **Useless Knowledge** and add it to the center region of the page. Again, the page will now appear as follows:

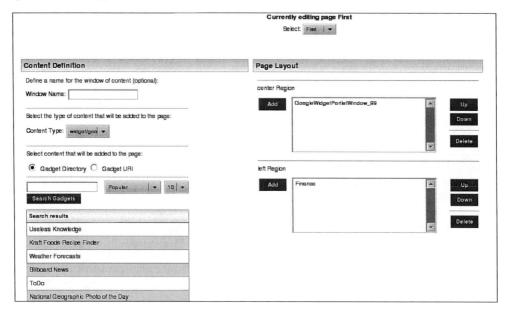

We are now ready to check out the new page that we created to customize our dashboard. Clicking on the **Dashboard** link takes us back to the dashboard page, and we can now see the new page **First**, along with the **Home** page.

Clicking on the new tab **First** will show the following page:

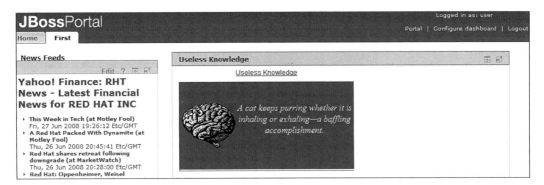

Our first portal page is now ready! As you can see, the content displayed is the content that we selected earlier, and is laid out in exactly the way that we wanted. We can continue to play with the options in the dashboard configuration screens, including different content types and page styles, to get to a page that makes us most efficient and productive with respect to information and functionality.

Summary

We had earlier talked about portals and portal servers in general. In this chapter, we introduced JBoss Portal Server 2.7.0 and its features. Most features are driven by current user needs, and the platform is built on a standards-based API that allows significant flexibility. We also talked in detail about the installation process of JBoss portal with emphasis on the differences and caveats for the various installation types offered, depending on the usage scenarios. A simplified installation and deployment process facilitates faster implementation and fewer problems, as demonstrated by the relatively immediate creation and management of pages on the platform.

We have only scratched the surface of the possibilities that exist in creating custom pages, leveraging the portlet API to create custom portlets, and to effectively manage enterprise content in order to enrich the portal pages further. In the next chapter, we will get started with creating portlets, the fundamental building blocks of a highly-functional portal server.

3
Saying Hello with a Portlet

JBoss portal server's primary strength lies in its ability to provide robust support for custom implementation of functionality using the portlet API. Portlets, the atomic unit of custom functionality, encompass the rich functionality and behavior we see aggregated on a portal web site.

In this chapter, we will try to understand the concepts and basics of building a functional portlet, by taking the traditional "Hello World" approach and building a portlet for it. The idea is to take a simple example and walk through the complete life cycle, from portlet development through to deployment, while introducing important concepts and configuration required for building a strong developmental foundation necessary for the complex use-cases introduced in the later chapters.

Portal page

Before we talk more about portlets, let us briefly refresh our perspective by looking at the broader picture of the relative positioning of portlets. In portals, a single aggregated set of information is displayed to the user using a portal page. A portal can have multiple portal pages. A portal page consists of various portlets with each contributing a page fragment or markup. Each portlet is a self-sufficient piece of functionality and is responsible for its own behavior and content. Each portlet resides in its own window and has its own controls. However, not all portlets necessarily have windows. There are some portlets that have pure content and no windows or controls.

When each portlet successfully executes and outputs a fragment, the portal page aggregates all of the content fragments from different portlets.

The following figure depicts all of the components of a portal page:

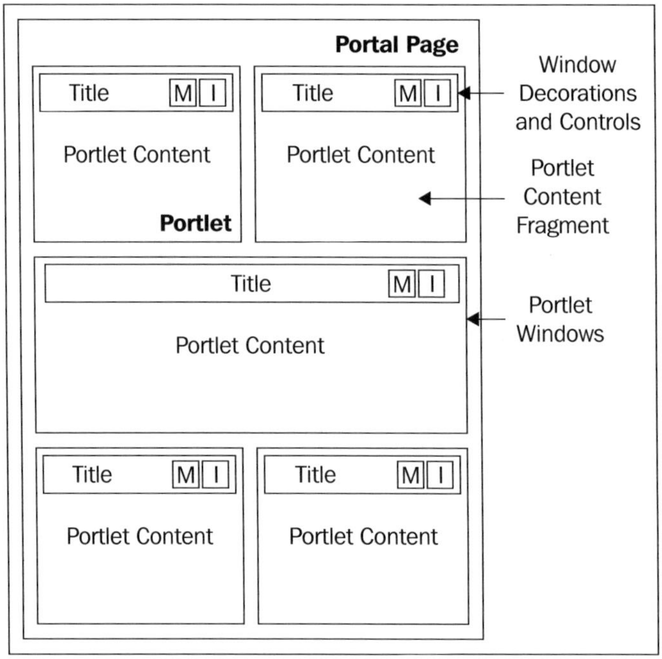

JSR-168 and JSR-286—Java portlet specification

Java Specification Request-168 is the foundational specification for building portlets. Similar to the servlet API, it is also the specification for portal server vendors to support portlets and applications built using the specification. The specification establishes standards for portlet interactions with portlet containers, and allows for compatibility with any portal server provider that adheres to to the standard.

The specification dictates the standards for deployment descriptors, deployment archives, base foundational classes, request processing, rendering, personalization, security, and so on. Given that the specification is the fundamental document for any portal development, it is a good idea to download it, read it, and use it as a reference. The documentation can be found on the Sun Microsystems web site: `http://jcp.org/en/jsr/detail?id=168`.

JSR-286 builds on JSR168, and is also called the **Portlet 2.0 specification**. As the portal platform matured, users started finding certain shortcomings in the existing portlet specification. These were specially in the areas of the portability of portlets, inter-portlet communication, events, filters, and resource serving. JBoss portal version 2.7.0 now provides support for JSR-286.

Portal URL

Portal URLs can become complicated as more pages are implemented. However, there are ways to set simpler alternate URLs, which make things a bit easier. It is important to note that portlets by themselves do not have a URL, and hence cannot be invoked directly. Portlets are part of a page and have an independent identity only from a browser perspective. Hence, they don't have their own URLs. Only portals and portal pages can be directly invoked; hence they can be invoked directly from browsers.

Each portal server can consist of several portals. Each one of these portals has its own URL. Similarly, each portal has several pages and each page has its own URL. To access a portal directly, we can use the portal name in the URL, which will then look like this: `http(s)://server:port/portal/<portal name>`.

Specifying only `/portal` takes us to the default portal. Similarly, to access a page on a given portal on the server, the URL we use is `/portal/<portal name>/<page name>`.

A **Content Management System (CMS)** serves content transparently like a portlet, hence doesn't impact the URL. We will discuss CMSs in more detail in Chapter 8.

Portlet modes

A portlet mode is a pointer to the type of function it will perform. There are three modes: VIEW, EDIT, and HELP. The mode indicates to a portlet the type of function it should perform and the associated content it should generate. When a portlet is invoked, the portlet is informed of the mode by the container. A portlet can have different modes depending on the function it needs to perform. There are three modes defined by the portlet specification, but a portal can extend them.

Let us look at these three modes in a bit more detail:

1. **VIEW**: This mode generates content and markup reflecting the current state of the portlet. It can be considered to be a read-only kind of a mode, where the content is presented for a user to read and interact with—but not necessarily to change. This mode is used for creating screens for a user to interact without editing any content, or for generating static content.

2. **EDIT**: Unlike VIEW mode, this mode allows a user to customize the behavior of the portlet. The portlet is supposed to provide options for the user to edit and customize the behavior of the portlet. This is typically used for creating and editing preferences.

3. **HELP**: This mode provides the user with helpful information related to the portlets usage. The information can be comprehensive or content-sensitive. This mode is not always required to be provided.

Window states

Window states relate to the space allocated for a given portlet on a page. As each portlet generates its markup, it is important to manage the real-estate of the aggregated final portal page effectively. Window states play a major role in this. Portal window states can be compared with the state of windows in a Microsoft Windows environment. A window in Windows can be minimized, maximized, or can be set as normal. Portal window states behave the same way. When the portlet is invoked, just like the portlet mode, the window state is also provided to the portlet. The portlet, based on the state provided, decides the best way to effectively organize the content in the portlet that will eventually be served as a fragment. Again, a portlet can change the state programmatically.

The three states defined by the specification are:

1. **NORMAL**: This indicates a shared space and requires a portlet to share the page with other portlets. The state is normal portal behavior, typically used when space is restricted and shared on the targeted device.

2. **MAXIMIZED**: This state indicates a broader freedom for the portlet to display its content. A portlet with this state can either be the only portlet displayed on this page, or one with a disproportionately higher amount of screen real-estate in comparison with other portlets displayed on the same page. This state is typically used for rich content display.

3. **MINIMIZED**: A kind of restricted viewing state that allows a portlet to display very little information, or in some cases, none at all.

A Hello World portlet

To understand the concepts better, let's dive right into writing the traditional "Hello World" code using a portlet.

By taking this simple example, we should be able to explore at least the major details of the specification, and their implication on real functioning code.

Portlet development environment

Portlet development, like web application development, requires a set of tools that help write code, build and successfully deploy our solution. The choice of the tools is very subjective, but typically, most of the developers prefer to use some kind of **Integrated Development Environment (IDE)** that encompasses all of their needs. However, if we want to stay agnostic of the IDE, command line developments can be a good option. At the least, the following set of tools is required to successfully create and deploy portlets:

- **Java Development Kit**: Any version above 1.4.2 is a good fit
- **Ant or Maven**: Either of these build tools can be leveraged to compile and build the application

Portlet package structure

Before we start with the code, let us build a context and briefly look at the overall structure of a deployable portlet archive.

Portlet archives are packaged as **WAR (Web Archive)** files, similar to archives in JEE applications. The content of our "Hello World" example as a WAR file will appear somewhat like this:

The directory structure is a standard structure for JEE projects. The structure can be created either manually or by using an IDE.

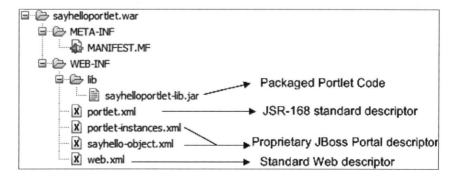

As you can see, the package consists of executable CLASS files, library JAR files and various deployment descriptors. For the purpose of simplicity, the example doesn't illustrate all of the scenarios, but a portlet WAR file can also consist of static content, resource bundles, JSPs, servlets, and so on.

The deployment descriptors illustrated in the figure are a combination of ones that are required by the JSR-286 specification, and others that are provided by JBoss to facilitate added features, easier configuration, and deployment on a JBoss portal platform. The JBoss-specific configurations provide significant value when deployed on a JBoss application server platform.

Writing the code

Now, let us look at the following code for our "Hello World" portlet:

```java
package org.jboss.portlet.hello;

import java.io.IOException;
import java.io.PrintWriter;

import javax.portlet.GenericPortlet;
import javax.portlet.PortletConfig;
import javax.portlet.PortletException;
import javax.portlet.RenderRequest;
import javax.portlet.RenderResponse;
import javax.portlet.UnavailableException;

public class HelloWorld extends GenericPortlet {
    public void init(PortletConfig portletConfig) throws
    UnavailableException, PortletException {
        super.init(portletConfig);
    }

    public void doView(RenderRequest request, RenderResponse
    response) throws PortletException, IOException {
        // set return content type
        response.setContentType("text/html");
        PrintWriter writer = response.getWriter();
        writer.println("<p>Hello World of Portals!</p>");
        writer.close();
    }
}
```

Let us parse through the code to understand it better.

```java
public class HelloWorld extends GenericPortlet {
```

JSR-168 requires every portlet to implement the `javax.portlet.Portlet` interface. The `Portlet` interface is used by the container to invoke the portlets in the container. The `GenericPortlet` class is the default implementation of the `Portlet` interface, and provides an abstract class that portlets can then extend, and override its methods for various functions. The method `processAction`, for example, is used to handle requests, and the `init` and `destroy` methods are used to manage the life cycle of the portlet. However, the `GenericPortlet` class is significant for its implementation of the `javax.portlet.Portlet render` method, which sets the title of the portlet and invokes the `doDispatch` method, which in turn delegates the processing to one of the portlet mode methods, based on the mode indicated by the request.

```
public void init(PortletConfig portletConfig) throws
UnavailableException, PortletException {
        super.init(portletConfig);
}
```

This is an optional method, but it is good practice to use it, and a convenient way to initialize the portlet with any configuration information. In this case, we are not using a special configuration; instead, we default to the parent implementation.

```
public void doView(RenderRequest request, RenderResponse response)
throws PortletException, IOException {
```

For our example, we have used only the `View` mode for our portlet. Hence, we need to implement only the `doView` method of the `GenericServlet` class. When the portlet is invoked, the `render` method invokes this `doView` method through the `doDispatch` method.

```
// set return content type
response.setContentType("text/html");
PrintWriter writer = response.getWriter();
writer.println("<p>Hello World of Portals!</p>");
```

Now that we have dispatched the request to the appropriate view mode, it is time to implement functionality in the portlet and send a response back.

As our response needs to be served to a browser, we first set the response type, `text/html` in this case. We then invoke the `PrintWriter` to output our message `Hello World of Portals!` in our portlet window.

This code generates the portlet fragment that will be aggregated with other fragments and content to generate the final page. Hence, it is important that the content that gets generated has tags that are valid inside an HTML `<body>` tag.

With this simple piece of code implementing our portlet functionality, we are now ready to tell our portlet container about the portlet.

Application descriptors

The application descriptors are XML-based configuration file options that, among other things, indicate the properties and behavior of the portlet to the container.

The portlet specification, JSR-286, mandates some of these options, while the rest are specific configurations mandated by the portal server — JBoss portal in our case. There is also a standard J2EE web deployment descriptor.

The following screenshot shows the descriptors as part of the deployable WAR file that we saw earlier:

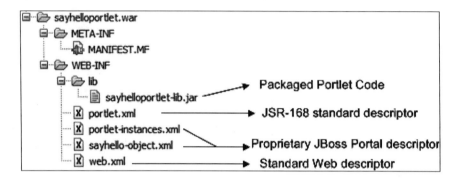

portlet.xml

`portlet.xml` is a mandatory deployment descriptor created as per the definitions in JSR-286 specification. All web related resources are defined in `web.xml`, as per the servlet specification, but all portal and portal server related resources are defined in `portlet.xml`.

```
<?xml version="1.0" encoding="UTF-8"?>
<portlet-app xmlns=http://java.sun.com/xml/ns/portlet/portlet-
                  app_2_0.xsd
             xmlns:xsi="http://www.w3.org/2001/XMLSchema-instance"
             xsi:schemaLocation="http://java.sun.com/xml/ns/portlet
                                 /portlet-app_2_0.xsd http://java.
                                 sun.com/xml/ns/portlet/portlet-
                                 app_2_0.xsd"
             version="2.0">
    <portlet>
       <portlet-name>SayHelloPortlet</portlet-name>
       <portlet-class>org.test.portlet.hello.SayHelloPortlet</portlet-
         class>
       <supports>
          <mime-type>text/html</mime-type>
```

```
        <portlet-mode>VIEW</portlet-mode>
    </supports>
    <portlet-info>
        <title>Say Hello Portlet</title>
    </portlet-info>
  </portlet>
</portlet-app>
```

Let's look at the descriptor at bit more closely:

```
<portlet-name>SayHelloPortlet</portlet-name>
```

This sets the name of the portlet. This name is a basic reference, and not the actual class name of the portlet.

```
<portlet-class>org.test.portlet.hello.SayHelloPortlet</portlet-class>
```

This is the actual implementation class of the portlet, and the field requires the fully-qualified name of the portlet class.

```
<supports>
        <mime-type>text/html</mime-type>
        <portlet-mode>VIEW</portlet-mode>
</supports>
```

This section describes the requested portlet modes for a given portlet, and the content types of the output to the render method.

By using the <mime-type> element, we are telling the render method that the portlet we are expecting to invoke will serve content of MIME type text/html, and the portlet mode for the portlet will be View. It is important to note that the portlet code should use the same mime type as the one declared here. We have used our output <mime-type> earlier in the code to be text/html, which matches with the type we have in the descriptor here.

```
<portlet-info>
        <title>Say Hello Portlet</title>
</portlet-info>
```

This section declares the title of the portlet window. Our portlet window on the final output page will be called Say Hello Portlet.

The portal window renderer uses this code to assign the window title. We have an option to override and assign a different title name in our code, but assigning the title in the descriptor is a fairly convenient.

portlet-instances.xml

`portlet-instances.xml` is JBoss-specific descriptor that facilitates the creation of multiple instances of the portlet. Creating multiple instances and assigning a unique `id` to each instance, allows us to customize and tailor the behavior of the same original portlet for different needs.

```xml
<?xml version="1.0" standalone="yes"?>
<deployments>
    <deployment>
        <instance>
            <instance-id>SayHelloPortletInstance</instance-id>
            <portlet-ref>SayHelloPortlet</portlet-ref>
        </instance>
    </deployment>
</deployments>
```

In our case, we are going to create only a single instance. We will name it `SayHelloPortletInstance`, and tie it to our portlet by using the name given in the `portlet.xml` file. The `<instance-id>` element can have any name, but the `<portlet-ref>` element should match the name specified in the `<portlet-name>` element in `portlet.xml`.

This file is primarily declaring new instances and tying these instances to a pre-existing portlet declaration. The associations and respective specifications are done in a different descriptor, named `*-object.xml`, where `*` can be any name. The element `<instance-id>` now gains significance, and is used to tie the instance to the `<instance-ref>` element in `*-object.xml`, as we will see in the next descriptor.

sayhello-object.xml

The `*-object.xml` defines the structure and configuration of a portlet instance that has been created earlier. We can use this file to create and configure windows and pages, their behavior, and their structure. We have decided to call our file, `sayhello-object.xml`:

```xml
<?xml version="1.0" encoding="UTF-8"?>
<deployments>
    <deployment>
        <if-exists>overwrite</if-exists>
        <parent-ref>default.default</parent-ref>
        <window>
            <window-name>SayHelloPortletWindow</window-name>
            <content>
                <content-type>portlet</content-type>
                <content-uri>SayHelloPortletInstance</content-uri>
            </content>
```

```
            <region>center</region>
            <height>1</height>
        </window>
    </deployment>
</deployments>
```

The descriptor allows for multiple deployments of portlets with distinct individual behaviors.

```
<if-exists>overwrite</if-exists>
```

This is used to manage copies of the object that may have already been instantiated. When we set the value to overwrite, we are telling the container to destroy any existing object and create a new one. If we set the value to the other allowed option, keep, the container retains any existing copy and creates a new instance. The decision to overwrite or keep an existing copy is purely a design call, and is based on the capacity of the server, performance requirements, and the complexity of the portlet.

```
<parent-ref>default.default</parent-ref>
```

This line basically indicates the location of our portlet, and stands for portal instance.portal page. In our case, by giving a value of default.default, we have decided to keep it simple and add the SayHelloPortlet to the default page of the default instance. We could very easily add the portlet to a new page that can be created using the approach outlined earlier in the chapter. In this case, the reference would change to default.newPage

```
<window-name>SayHelloPortletWindow</window-name>
```

This line assigns an arbitrary but unique window name to the portlet window.

```
<instance-ref>SayHelloPortletInstance</instance-ref>
```

This line references the portlet instance created in the portlet-instance.xml file. Again, the value of this element should be the same as the <instance-id> element in portlet-instance.xml

```
<region>center</region>
<height>1</height>
```

These lines specify the location and dimension of the portlet window. There are various configuration options for these elements, but in our case, we are indicating that the portlet should appear in the center of the page layout as described by identifier in the layout descriptor, and should be second portlet from the top as indicated by height 1. Height "0" is the first portlet from the top in a column. We will see later how the location and the order can be changed using the admin console.

The inter-relationship of these descriptors is as follows:

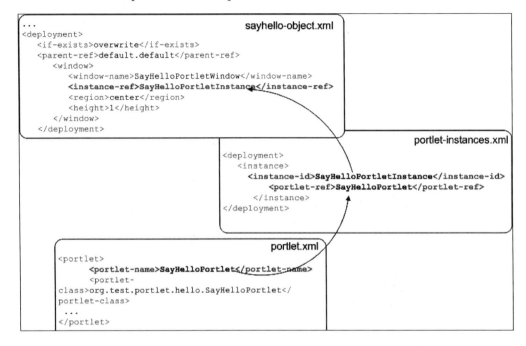

The `<portlet-name>` in `portlet.xml` is used to create an instance using `<instance-id>` in `portlet-instances.xml`. The properties of this instance is defined in `*-object.xml`.

web.xml

`web.xml` is a standard web deployment descriptor mandated by the servlet specification, and any web resource configurations go in this file.

Due to the simplicity of our example, in our case, this file is empty.

Building the application

Now that we have our code and descriptors in place, let us start building our deployable artifact, and plan for its eventual deployment on the server.

The source code associated with this chapter provides the necessary build scripts to compile and create deployable artifacts. There are multiple ways of creating the WAR file—the build script uses one such technique. We will create our portlet source file under the `src/main` directory, and place our deployment descriptors under `src/resource/sayhelloportlet-war`. The libraries required for building will go under the `lib` directory.

The script will first compile the source, create a JAR file of the compiled binaries, and copy this JAR file to the `src/resource/sayhelloportlet-war/WEB-INF/lib` directory. It will then package the contents of the `src/resource/sayhelloportlet-war` directory into a WAR file.

The screen output will look like the following screenshot:

```
C:\WINXP\system32\cmd.exe                                    _ □ X

C:\projects\SayHelloPortlet>ant build
Buildfile: build.xml

prepare:

build:
    [javac] Compiling 1 source file to C:\projects\SayHelloPortlet\output\classe
s
      [jar] Building jar: C:\projects\SayHelloPortlet\output\lib\sayhelloportlet
-lib.jar
     [copy] Copying 1 file to C:\projects\SayHelloPortlet\src\resources\sayhello
portlet-war\WEB-INF\lib
      [jar] Building jar: C:\projects\SayHelloPortlet\sayhelloportlet.war

BUILD SUCCESSFUL
Total time: 1 second
C:\projects\SayHelloPortlet>
```

Although we have packaged the portlet classes as a library, it is not necessary to do so. As with a J2EE application, the CLASS file tree can be copied as it is, below the `WEB-INF/classes` directory.

Deploying the application

We are now ready to deploy the WAR file to the portal server. We can deploy the file in a couple of ways:

- Deploy as a single WAR file archive
- Deploy in an exploded mode where the contents retain their directory structure

An exploded deployment has significant value when we need more control over the content. However, for our purposes, we will use the WAR file deployment option.

To deploy the WAR file, all we need to do is drop the file into the deploy directory of the JBoss application server (AS or EAP). This can be done as a hot deploy, while the server is running.

For bundle installs, the deploy directory is `$JBOSS_PORTAL_HOME/server/default/deploy`.

The output on the console, indicating deployment activity after we drop the WAR file, is as follows:

```
03:27:42,810 INFO  [TomcatDeployer] deploy, ctxPath=/sayhelloportlet,
warUrl=.../tmp/deploy/tmp26738sayhelloportlet-exp.war/
```

Accessing the page and portal URL

Once we have successfully deployed the application, we can then go to the default URL for JBoss server: `http://localhost:8080/portal`.

The default URL and page corresponds to our `default.default` location setting earlier in the descriptor.

We can now see our portal, displayed in the center of the page, in **View** mode:

Minor changes to content can be done directly on the tree without redeploying the whole archive. To trigger a redeploy, we just need to update the timestamp on the `web.xml` file by touching it. A `web.xml` file with a timestamp later than the last deployment will trigger the JBoss portal to deploy the application again. It is worth noting here that this time the deployment takes place in an exploded format as there is no WAR file involved.

Summary

In this chapter, we went a bit deeper into JBoss portal server and tried to understand portlets better by creating a simple portlet application. We went through the complete life cycle, from code creation to deployment. Hopefully, this overview tour gave you a good idea of the major components that are required to create a functional portlet.

This introductory application barely touched the true potential of the server and the choices it offers. In the coming chapters, we will explore the potential of the portal further; we will develop custom portlets, and move into some real world scenarios by introducing some newer patterns, choices, and techniques.

Nothing clears things up better than a demo application. In the next chapter, we will also introduce the sample application—a corporate Intranet portal called "MyCompany Portal", which we will use throughout this book. As we learn new concepts, we will add them to the portal, and it should hopefully jump-start our enterprise portal development.

4
Managing the View

Our simple example in the last chapter demonstrated how a portlet functions, and described the various components that assist in the successful deployment and delivery of the portlet. However, realistic enterprise portal solutions perform complex functions, and users have diverse needs. This requires us to use tools and techniques that make our implementation quick, efficient and robust.

In this chapter, we will focus on views and presentation tier technologies. The presentation tier is the segment of the application that is responsible for building content that directly interacts with the user. Hence, it should be dynamic, flexible to changing tastes, and loosely coupled to the core business functions of the application. Starting with template-based implementations using **Java Server Pages (JSP)**, we will eventually move on to use a component-based technique such as **Java Server Faces (JSF)**.

We will then use all of this to build our example "MyCompany" intranet portal. We will create custom portlets using the view technologies, and add features to the portal application.

The Presentation tier in portals

Before we go into implementing views, let us spend some time talking about the various presentation tier view options that we have.

The presentation tier provides a direct interaction with the users of the application. Hence, it should be flexible, efficient, and easy to implement and adapt. There are many ways to implement the presentation tier view in a portal. JSP, JSF, and so on, provide a varied set of options for the successful implementation of a product or service.

In subsequent sections of this chapter, we will discuss the implementation of the presentation tier view in portlets on a JBoss portal server. Each implementation offers certain advantages. The choice of a given technology depends on factors such as the size of the application, its complexity, and the cost of implementing it.

Using Java Server Pages

Creating a HTML markup directly in portlets is okay for simple applications such as our "Hello World" example. However, for useful, real-world applications, we need a more comprehensive solution. The portlet specification allows the delegation of content creation and rendering to servlets and JSPs. JSPs are the template-based implementation standards for J2EE application development. They provide the flexibility and features required for developing the rich views that today's web sites need. A portal can leverage the strengths of JSPs, such as separation of markup from logic, powerful tag libraries, and so on, and create a robust and scalable solution.

Let us build a portlet, using JSP, that performs the simple task of prompting for a name and returning a greeting.

Archive package structure with JSP

The following WAR package structure explicitly displays the JSPs that are used for rendering the view. The `portlet` class, here packaged in the `jar` library file, leverages the JSPs to interact with the portal to create the view.

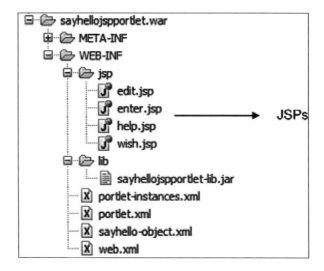

Writing the code

Using JSP allows the separation of executable content from its presentation. Hence, the portlet class now contains logic that needs to be performed both before and after the portlet is rendered on the screen. The portlet class contains no markup or any other view-specific code. It plainly refers to the JSPs, which in turn are responsible for creating the view.

Portlet class

The `portlet` class is responsible for the execution of functionality, and the invocation of appropriate JSP view pages. The `portlet` class is shown in the following code listing:

```java
package org.test.portlet.hello;

import java.io.IOException;
import java.io.PrintWriter;

import javax.portlet.ActionRequest;
import javax.portlet.ActionResponse;
import javax.portlet.GenericPortlet;
import javax.portlet.PortletConfig;
import javax.portlet.PortletException;
import javax.portlet.PortletRequestDispatcher;
import javax.portlet.RenderRequest;
import javax.portlet.RenderResponse;
import javax.portlet.UnavailableException;

public class SayHelloJSPPortlet extends GenericPortlet {
    public void init(PortletConfig portletConfig) throws
    UnavailableException,
            PortletException {
        super.init(portletConfig);
    }

    public void doView(RenderRequest request, RenderResponse
    response)
            throws PortletException, IOException {

        // set return content type
        response.setContentType("text/html");

      String name= (String) request.getParameter("name");

      if(name != null || name == "") {
         PortletRequestDispatcher reqDispatcher = getPortletContext()
                    .getRequestDispatcher("/WEB-INF/jsp/wish.jsp");
         request.setAttribute("name", name);
         reqDispatcher.include(request, response);
      } else {
         PortletRequestDispatcher reqDispatcher = getPortletContext()
                    .getRequestDispatcher("/WEB-INF/jsp/enter.jsp");
         reqDispatcher.include(request, response);
         }
    }

public void processAction(ActionRequest actionRequest,
ActionResponse actionResponse) throws PortletException, IOException,
UnavailableException
```

```
    {
        String name = (String) actionRequest.getParameter("name");

        // send name back to view
        actionResponse.setRenderParameter("name", name);
    }
    protected void doHelp(RenderRequest renderRequest, RenderResponse
    renderResponse) throws PortletException, IOException,
    UnavailableException
    {
        renderResponse.setContentType("text/html");
        PortletRequestDispatcher reqDispatcher = getPortletContext()
                    .getRequestDispatcher("/WEB-INF/jsp/help.jsp");
        reqDispatcher.include(renderRequest, renderResponse);
    }
    protected void doEdit(RenderRequest renderRequest, RenderResponse
    renderResponse) throws PortletException, IOException,
    UnavailableException
    {
        renderResponse.setContentType("text/html");
        PortletRequestDispatcher reqDispatcher = getPortletContext()
                    .getRequestDispatcher("/WEB-INF/jsp/edit.jsp");
        reqDispatcher.include(renderRequest, renderResponse);
    }
}
```

Let us look at the important segments individually:

```
public void processAction(ActionRequest actionRequest,
ActionResponse actionResponse) throws PortletException, IOException,
UnavailableException
    {
        String name = (String) actionRequest.getParameter("name");
        // send name back to view
        actionResponse.setRenderParameter("name", name);
    }
```

The method accepts a request from the browser and extracts the entered name.

```
if(name != null || name == "") {
        PortletRequestDispatcher reqDispatcher = getPortletContext()
                    .getRequestDispatcher("/WEB-INF/jsp/wish.jsp");
        request.setAttribute("name", name);
        reqDispatcher.include(request, response);
    }
    else {
```

```
        PortletRequestDispatcher reqDispatcher = getPortletContext()
                    .getRequestDispatcher("/WEB-INF/jsp/enter.jsp");
        reqDispatcher.include(request, response);
}
```

When a request first comes to the class, we check for the value entered, from the view. If one exists, it means that the user has submitted a name, and we take the user to the wish.jsp page. But if it is empty or null, we send the screen on which the user can enter the values back to the user.

```
protected void doHelp(RenderRequest renderRequest, RenderResponse
renderResponse) throws PortletException, IOException,
UnavailableException

. . .

    protected void doEdit(RenderRequest renderRequest, RenderResponse
renderResponse) throws PortletException, IOException,
UnavailableException
```

These two methods offer additional functions depending on the mode values defined in the application descriptor.

JSPs and portlet tags

Tags are one of the major features of JSP specifications. Repetitive pieces of code to implement the same functionality complicate pages unnecessarily, and make them prone to errors. Encapsulating these repeated functions in a tag library, and then passing parameters to them allows for cleaner and more maintainable implementations of JSPs. Due to the portable nature of the tags, it is also easy to build or provide third-party tags that can enhance the richness of the JSP's capability.

JBoss portal comes with its own set of standard tags that can be leveraged to make portlet development easier and more efficient.

Let's look at the use of tags in the enter.jsp file:

```
<%@ taglib uri="http://java.sun.com/portlet" prefix="portlet" %>

<portlet:defineObjects/>

<div align="center">
    Using JSP for portal view. Please enter your name!
    <br/>
    <form action="<portlet:actionURL><portlet:param name="page"
     value="view"/></portlet:actionURL>" method="POST">
        Name:  <input type="text" name="name"/>
    </form>
    <br/>
</div>
```

The useful `portlet` tag library is one of the main advantages of using JSPs. The tag libraries are provided by default by JBoss portal, and hence, need not be included.

```
<portlet:defineObjects/>
```

The `defineObjects` tag provides the page with `renderRequest`, `actionRequest`, and `portletConfig`, through which the page can retrieve the information it needs.

```
<form action="<portlet:actionURL><portlet:param name="page"
value="view"/></portlet:actionURL>" method="POST">
```

This entry uses the `taglib` to define the URL that will be used for submission of form information. The form is directly submitted to `processAction` on the portal.

```
<%@ taglib uri="http://java.sun.com/portlet" prefix="portlet" %>
<portlet:defineObjects/>

<div align="center">
   Hi, <%= renderRequest.getAttribute("name") %>! Welcome!
   <br/>
   <a href="<portlet:renderURL></portlet:renderURL>">Back</a>
</div>
```

Similar to the request submission, the `renderURL` `taglib` can be an effective solution for rendering views and displaying information. The `<portlet:renderURL>` can be used to connect directly to the `doView` method.

Application descriptors

The application descriptor, `portlet.xml`, is as follows:

```
<portlet-app
xmlns="http://java.sun.com/xml/ns/portlet/portlet-app_2_0.xsd"
xmlns:xsi="http://www.w3.org/2001/XMLSchema-instance"           xsi:
schemaLocation="http://java.sun.com/xml/ns/portlet/portlet-app_2_0.xsd
http://java.sun.com/xml/ns/portlet/portlet-app_2_0.xsd"
            version="2.0">
   <portlet>
      <portlet-name>SayHelloJSPPortlet</portlet-name>
      <portlet-class>
            org.test.portlet.hello.SayHelloJSPPortlet</portlet-class>
      <supports>
         <mime-type>text/html</mime-type>
         <portlet-mode>VIEW</portlet-mode>
         <portlet-mode>EDIT</portlet-mode>
         <portlet-mode>HELP</portlet-mode>
      </supports>
```

```
        <portlet-info>
           <title>Say Hello JSP Portlet</title>
        </portlet-info>
     </portlet>
</portlet-app>
```

The `portlet.xml` file defines the portlet and sets the modes of operation for the portlet. In our case, the portlet operates in the VIEW, EDIT, and HELP modes.

The `sayhello-object.xml` file declares the location of the portlet instance defined in `portlet-instance.xml`.

As we can see in the following code, in the `<parent-ref>` section, we want to add our JSP test portlet directly onto the default home page of the default portal instance:

```
<?xml version="1.0" encoding="UTF-8"?>
<deployments>
   <deployment>
      <if-exists>overwrite</if-exists>
      <parent-ref>default.default</parent-ref>
      <window>
         <window-name>SayHelloJSPPortletWindow</window-name>
         <instance-ref>SayHelloJSPPortletInstance</instance-ref>
         <region>center</region>
         <height>1</height>
      </window>
   </deployment>
</deployments>
```

Building the application

The process for building the application is pretty much the same as a regular implementation, only in this case the JSPs are in their own directories and are packaged together at the end of the build. The `ant` script that is provided with the code builds the code, and the output of this is as follows:

Deploying the application

As seen in the following screenshot, when the page is loaded, the new JSP-based portlet shows up at the bottom of the page. The portlet can now be tested by submitting a name, upon which the server returns the `wish.jsp` page along with a greeting.

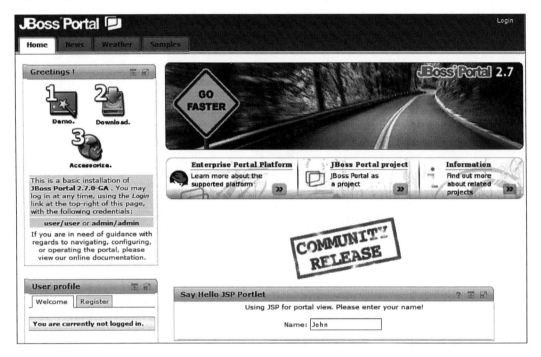

When the form is submitted, the portal processes the request, giving us back the `wish.jsp` file, along with the greeting as shown in the following screenshot:

Now, let's look at an alternative view implementation, using Java Server Faces.

Using Java Server Faces

JSF is another popular user interface or view framework for Java-based web applications. JSF is an evolution of JSP, and is intended to reduce the complexity and increase the capability of view implementations. It is built around the concept of component architecture for views, which allows enhanced re-usability, state management, event generation, and extensibility. With a gamut of tools available today for JSF, implementing feature-rich user interfaces by using JSF is significantly easier than by using traditional JSPs.

However, implementing views using JSF in portals is not as straightforward. JSF request processing and page rendering are very different from how a portlet environment processes requests and renders pages. This is largely due to the fundamental architectural differences in the implementation of the technologies. Hence, custom APIs have to be written to blend the two technologies together. However, efforts are underway to standardize such an implementation.

JSR -301 Portlet Bridge

Currently, every JSF implementation provides binaries that manage the execution of JSF in a portlet environment. The JSR-301 Portlet Bridge specification for JSF is a formal effort to standardize the space and specify a clear standard for the implementation of bridges between portlets and JSF.

A high-level overview of the JSF Portlet Bridge and its relationship to portal and JSF implementation is shown in the following figure, adapted from the JSR-301 specification.

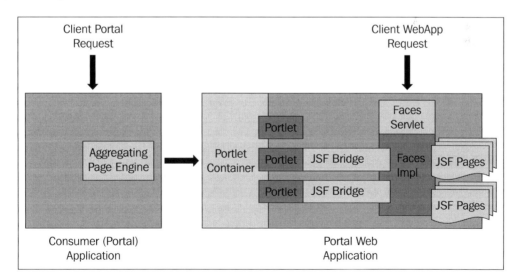

Package structure with JSF

Just as we did with the JSP-based portlet, let's recreate the application using JSF.

The WAR file package structure of a JSF-based implementation appears as shown in the following screenshot. For our implementation, we have taken the Apache MyFaces implementation of JSF as an example.

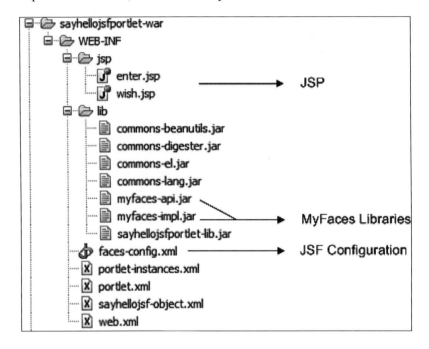

Most of the files here are the same as in the JSP implementation, except for the `faces-config.xml` and the `MyFaces` library files. The JSPs are still used for rendering content, but the life cycle of the view is managed through JSF-based user interface components.

Another interesting aspect is the absence of the `portlet` class. A single `bean` class, using the user interface, takes care of the implementation.

Application descriptors

```
<?xml version="1.0"?>
<!DOCTYPE faces-config PUBLIC
    "-//Sun Microsystems, Inc.//DTD JavaServer Faces Config 1.0//EN"
    "http://java.sun.com/dtd/web-facesconfig_1_0.dtd">
<faces-config>
```

```
<managed-bean>
    <description>Name Bean</description>
    <managed-bean-name>name</managed-bean-name>
    <managed-bean-class>
        org.test.portlet.hello.Name
    </managed-bean-class>
    <managed-bean-scope>session</managed-bean-scope>
</managed-bean>

<navigation-rule>
    <navigation-case>
        <from-outcome>done</from-outcome>
        <to-view-id>/WEB-INF/jsp/wish.jsp</to-view-id>
    </navigation-case>
</navigation-rule>
</faces-config>
```

The MyFaces configuration file defines the request, response, and values required for a successful implementation. The file lists the outcome and the navigation rules once the request starts to be processed. The managed bean is defined, and its state is managed by the container.

```
<?xml version="1.0" encoding="UTF-8"?>
<portlet-app xmlns="http://java.sun.com/xml/ns/portlet/portlet-
                    app_2_0.xsd"
            xmlns:xsi="http://www.w3.org/2001/XMLSchema-instance"
            xsi:schemaLocation="http://java.sun.com/xml/ns/portlet/
                        portlet-app_1_0.xsd http://java.sun.com/
                        xml/ns/portlet/portlet-app_2_0.xsd"
            version="2.0">
    <portlet>
        <portlet-name>SayHelloJSFPortlet</portlet-name>
        <portlet-class>
          org.apache.myfaces.portlet.MyFacesGenericPortlet
        </portlet-class>
        <init-param>
            <name>default-view</name>
            <value>/WEB-INF/jsp/enter.jsp</value>
        </init-param>
        <supports>
            <mime-type>text/html</mime-type>
            <portlet-mode>VIEW</portlet-mode>
        </supports>
        <portlet-info>
            <title>Say Hello JSF Portlet</title>
        </portlet-info>
    </portlet>
</portlet-app>
```

Let's go through the important parts of the descriptor:

```
<portlet-name>SayHelloJSFPortlet</portlet-name>
    <portlet-class>
        org.apache.myfaces.portlet.MyFacesGenericPortlet
    </portlet-class>
```

The `portlet.xml` file now references the `MyFacesGenericPortlet` implementation, as opposed to `GenericServlet`.

```
<init-param>
        <name>default-view</name>
        <value>/WEB-INF/jsp/enter.jsp</value>
    </init-param>
```

We also define the default view, which tells the container to always show this page first.

Apart from the above configurations, there is a small configuration required in `web.xml`:

```
<web-app>
    <context-param>
        <param-name>
            org.jboss.jbossfaces.WAR_BUNDLES_JSF_IMPL
        </param-name>
        <param-value>true</param-value>
    </context-param>
</web-app>
```

This entry notifies the container that the application archive carries its own libraries, so that there are no class path conflicts. For more information, please refer to `http://www.jboss.org/community/docs/DOC-10182`.

We also add an entry to `web.xml` that indicates to the JBoss portal that the application WAR carries its own JSF implementation libraries. This ensures that there are no conflicts between the JSF libraries that already come packaged with the server.

```
<web-app>
    <context-param>
        <param-name>
            org.jboss.jbossfaces.WAR_BUNDLES_JSF_IMPL
        </param-name>
        <param-value>true</param-value>
    </context-param>
</web-app>
```

The value of the configuration variable `WAR_BUNDLES_JSF_IMPL` is set to `True`.

Building the application

All of the relevant libraries are added to the `lib` directory. The application is built just like any other application, and the outcome is a WAR file.

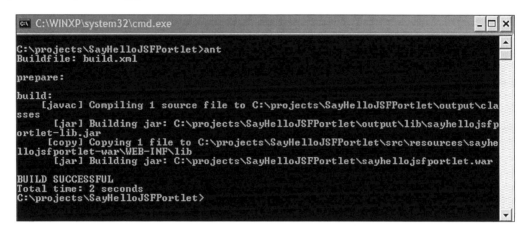

Deploying the application

The deployment is pretty straightforward, and by opening the URL in the browser, we can see a fully functional portlet implementation at the bottom of the page.

When the form is completed and submitted, the page refreshes to provide the following response:

Using JBoss Seam

While on JSF, another interesting framework for portlet implementation is **JBoss Seam**. Seam is a robust end-to-end application solution. Views of Seam form a small part of the whole implementation. Maximum value can be extracted if we seamlessly integrate a portal view with a Seam view. However, if we decide to implement JBoss Seam application in a JBoss portal server, it will require the latest JSF Portlet Bridge. Currently, the bridge is in beta phase, but it supports most of the features of Seam and can be used effectively in a portlet environment. When available as a general release, the bridge will allow almost seamless transitions to the portal environment.

We have seen how portlets can be easily built and deployed to the portal platform using JSP and JSF. It is also very easy to extend the implementation of views to various other frameworks, such as Struts2, Spring MVC, and so on, to provide a robust portlet implementation.

Building a sample application: an intranet portal

Now that we have learnt the basics of creating views and portal pages, let us try and apply them. In the next few sections, we will create a sample application that mimics a typical corporate intranet portal that is serving users within the company. We will continue to build on this example in the coming chapters, when we learn about other capabilities of the JBoss portal server.

Our intranet application is purely for demonstration purposes, and although it is intended to mimic a typical corporate intranet portal's behavior, is not as feature-rich as a real-world portal would be, for obvious reasons. The idea is to develop a portal that incorporates the major learning points from the chapters in this book. Hopefully, the concepts will be clear enough for you to extend the portal, and build bigger and better features.

Introduction

The portal will initially consist of at least two pages. The default home page of the portal will have a few portlets related to the user, along with a portlet that we will build using JSP. The second page will have a collection of utility tools for the user of the portal.

For simplicity, we will use the portal server admin console to set up the portal instance and initialize a few pages. This will also help us better understand the admin console features. Please note that setup up portal instance and defining new pages can all be done using deployment descriptors as we will briefly review later.

Creating the MyCompany portal

Before we talk about portlets, we need to first create a portal, configure it, and add some pages to it. We will use the admin console to do this.

1. Log in to the admin console, using **admin** as both the admin userID and password.
2. Click on the **Admin** link in the top right navigation area. We will now be on the **Portlet Objects** section of the admin page, with an option to create a new portal.
3. You'll notice that there is already a portal, named **default**, which is set as the default portal when we log into JBoss portal server for the first time. Let's create a new portal and name it **mycompany**. Click on **Make Default**, if you want this new portal to be the default portal on the server.

4. Now let's add a few pages to our portal. We will create two pages to get things going. Click on the **mycompany** link. We always get an initial first page when we create a new portal. This is titled **default**. Let's create a new page called **Tools**.

As mentioned earlier, we can achieve the same configuration by adding the following in the deployment descriptor `mycompany-object.xml`.

```xml
<?xml version="1.0" encoding="UTF-8"?>
<deployments>
    <deployment>
        <if-exists>overwrite</if-exists>
        <parent-ref/>
         <portal>
           <portal-name>mycompany</portal-name>
         <page>
               <page-name>default</page-name>
           </page>
            <page>
                  <page-name>Tools</page-name>
            </page>
        </portal>
    </deployment>
</deployments>
```

This will create a new portal by name mycompany and create two pages called default and Tools.

A JSP portlet

Now that we have the portal server set up with our portal definition, let's create a sample JSP-based portlet to add to it. We will later add some other portlets to our **default** and **Tools** pages, to make the portal a bit more functional.

Let's create a custom portlet with the basic functionality of showing the tasks for the day when a user logs on. The user can click on a task and see its details. Please note that the portlet is for understanding the concepts, and all of the features are not functional. It is left for you to make these features come alive.

First, let's create the portlet class:

```
org.mycompany.portlet.hello.ViewPortlet.java.
public class ViewPortlet extends GenericPortlet {
    private PortletContext portletContext;
    // Add all logic related to submitted forms, responses and
       actions
    // Pretty much default method for all functions, except edit and
       help
    public void init(PortletConfig config) throws PortletException {
        super.init(config);
        portletContext = config.getPortletContext();
    }

    public void doView(RenderRequest request,RenderResponse response)
        throws PortletException,IOException {
        String contentPage = getContentJSP(request);
        response.setContentType(request.getResponseContentType());
        if (contentPage != null && contentPage.length() != 0) {
          try {
            PortletRequestDispatcher dispatcher = portletContext.
                                          getRequestDispatcher
                                          (contentPage);
            dispatcher.include(request, response);
          } catch (IOException e) {
            throw new PortletException("ViewPortlet.doView
            exception", e);
          }
        }
    }
    // Use this method to add logic to "Edit" function
```

```
// For example, show the appropriate edit page
// Note: Any actions when the edit page is submitted, go in the
   doView() method
public void doEdit(RenderRequest request,RenderResponse response)
    throws PortletException {
    String editPage = getEditJSP(request);
    response.setContentType(request.getResponseContentType());
    if (editPage != null && editPage.length() != 0) {
      try {
        PortletRequestDispatcher dispatcher = portletContext.
                                  getRequestDispatcher(editPage);
        dispatcher.include(request, response);
      } catch (IOException e) {
          throw new PortletException("ViewPortlet.doEdit
          exception", e);
      }
    }
}

// Use this method to add logic to "Help" function
// For example, show the appropriate help page, based on context
 public void doHelp(RenderRequest request,RenderResponse response)
    throws PortletException {
    String helpPage = getHelpJSP(request);
response.setContentType(request.getResponseContentType());
    if (helpPage != null && helpPage.length() != 0) {
      try {
        PortletRequestDispatcher dispatcher = portletContext.
                                  getRequestDispatcher(helpPage);
        dispatcher.include(request, response);
      } catch (IOException e) {
          throw new PortletException("ViewPortlet.doHelp
          exception", e);
      }
    }
}

public void processAction (ActionRequest request, ActionResponse
                          actionResponse)
throws PortletException, java.io.IOException {

  actionResponse.setRenderParameters(request.getParameterMap());
}

protected String getContentJSP(RenderRequest request) throws
PortletException {

String page = (String) request.getParameter("page");
```

```
        if(page != null && page.equals("reviewtasks")) {
            return "/WEB-INF/jsp/reviewtasks.jsp";
        } else {
            return "/WEB-INF/jsp/content.jsp";
          }
        }

        protected String getEditJSP(RenderRequest request) throws
        PortletException {
            return "/WEB-INF/jsp/edit.jsp";
        }

        protected String getHelpJSP(RenderRequest request) throws
        PortletException {
            return "/WEB-INF/jsp/help.jsp";
        }
}
```

As you can see in the above code, the content page displays a default set of tasks, and when a task page is requested, the appropriate page is shown.

There is also code to deal with the **Edit** and **Help** option, which gets triggered when a user clicks on the links provided by the portal on the portlet.

A snippet of the `content.jsp` file invoked when the portlet loads, is as follows:

```
<%@ taglib uri="http://java.sun.com/portlet" prefix="portlet" %>
<%@ page session="false" %>

<portlet:defineObjects/>
<portlet:renderURL var="rURL">
</portlet:renderURL>

<table>
  <tr valign=top>
    <td>
      Today is
    </td>
    <td nowrap>
    <% DateFormat df = DateFormat.getDateTimeInstance
                        (DateFormat.FULL, DateFormat.SHORT,
                        Locale.getDefault()); %>
    <%=df.format(new Date())%>
    </td>
    <td> </td>
  </tr>
  <tr valign=top>
   <td>
```

```
      <B>Tasks For the Day: </B>
     </td>
    </tr>
  </TABLE>
  <%@ include file="tasks.jsp" %>
```

The `content.jsp` file is the default view for the portlet, and in turn includes other files, such as `tasks.jsp`, to render its full content.

The source code accompanying this book provides details of the remaining JSPs.

The `*-object.xml` application descriptor, named `mycompany-object.xml`, in the `WEB-INF` directory needs to include the entry for the location of the portlet on the server pages.

```
<?xml version="1.0" encoding="UTF-8"?>
<deployments>
   <deployment>
      <if-exists>overwrite</if-exists>
      <parent-ref/>
       <portal>
         <portal-name>mycompany</portal-name>
       <page>
             <page-name>default</page-name>
          <window>
                <window-name>ViewPortletWindow</window-name>
                <instance-ref>ViewPortletInstance</instance-ref>
                <region>right</region>
                <height>1</height>
          </window>
        </page>
        <page>
             <page-name>Tools</page-name>
        </page>
      </portal>
   </deployment>
</deployments>
```

The `ViewPortletWindow` is now assigned to the `default` page on the `mycompany` portal. All other application descriptors remain pretty much the same as in the JSP example we discussed earlier, with appropriate edits to reference `ViewPortlet`.

Now, let's build the code using the provided build script. The WAR file is deployed on the server, and the portal is accessed through its default URL at `http://localhost:8080/portal`.

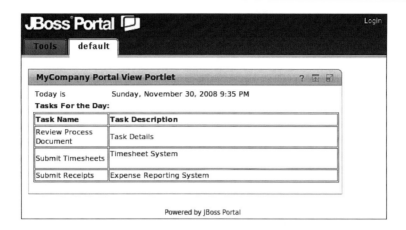

The portlet is loaded into the default page of the **MyCompany** portal. We haven't yet logged in, hence we don't see the **Edit** link. We can also see the **Tools** page we created earlier.

Now that we have the portlet working on the default page, let's go back to our **Admin** screen and add some more portlets on the page, to make it look like a functional portal.

We will use a couple of existing canned portlets provided by the server, and add these to the left of the page on the layout, as shown in the following screenshot:

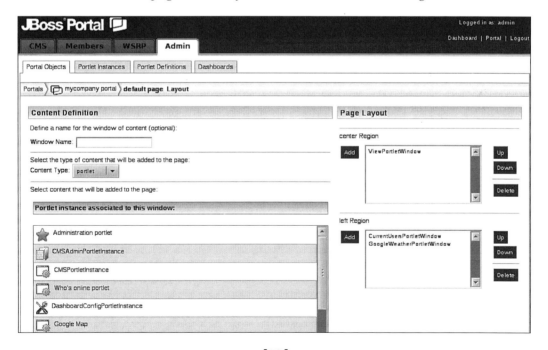

The leftmost side of the default page will have a portlet that displays current users, and another portlet below it that shows the weather. Please note that we are adding the portlets just to decorate the page for now. If these portlets are not added to the deployment descriptor mentioned earlier, they will be removed when we deploy the application the next time.

While we are here, we will also edit the layout of the **Tools** page, and add a few portlets to it, containing tools are helpful that for any user.

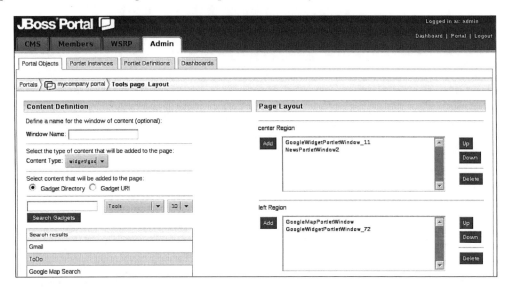

Going back to our portal home page, we should see all of the changes that we have made. Let's log in as the test user, using **user** as both the userID and the password.

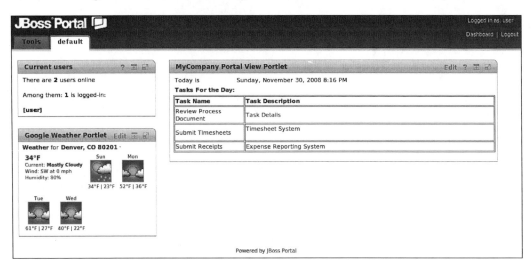

Clicking on the **Task Details** link, we can now see the page generated by `viewtasks.jsp`. As we have logged in, we can now also see the **Edit** link.

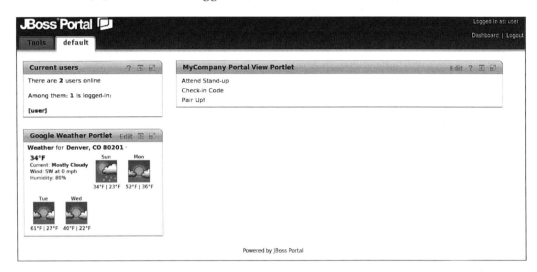

The portal now consists of two pages: the **default** page (the screen that we have just used) and the **Tools** page. The portlets added to the **Tools** page are now available for use.

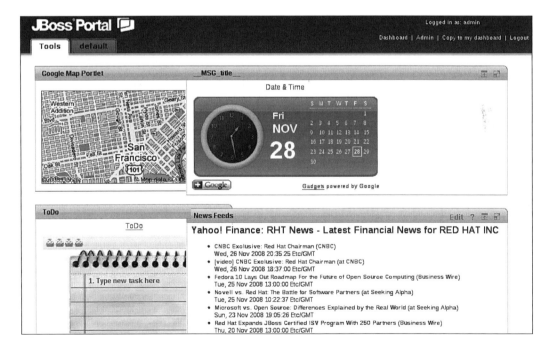

Hopefully, this example has provided enough perspective and depth for you to start creating portal applications using JSP-based views. The approach is pretty much the same even if we choose to use a JSF-based implementation. The JSF example we saw earlier in the chapter is a good reference. In later chapters, we will look at other alternatives, such as a content management system that will help us create pages with static content in a much easier fashion.

Summary

In this chapter, we reviewed the various options that are available for effectively managing the presentation in portlets using technologies such as JSP, JSF, and so on. We also saw a few examples of each of these technologies. Each view technology needs its own set of deployment descriptors and executables. With the implementation of portal-JSF bridges and so on, the standalone applications can be now migrated easily to the portal environment.

To understand the concepts better, we also created a portal application from scratch, and added a custom portlet that we created with JSP-based views.

In the next chapter, we will look at how we can customize and personalize our own portal. Personalization is one of the hallmarks of portal. A server that offers higher personalization capability tends to provide significantly higher returns for the customers of the portals.

5
Personalizing Our Portal Experience

Portals are designed to reach out and interact with users through convenient and efficient means. The usability of the portal and its broader acceptance as a tool of choice for most operations can be further enhanced by creating content that treats every user distinctly and provides choices and options that are specific to that particular user.

Content personalization allows for such granular treatment of individual users and caters to their specific preferences for using the portal platform. In this chapter, we will discuss how the portal servers can be effectively leveraged to personalize and customize content including portlets, creating an application that communicates to the users in a form that is most convenient and personal to them.

Personalization and customization

Sometimes, the terms personalization and customization are used interchangeably. However, there is a difference. Personalization is a lot closer to a user's interaction preferences, and is a process in which the container anticipates and interprets a user's needs by processing information about the user behind the scenes and then generating the page accordingly. A user doesn't typically expect a personalized page, and hence doesn't explicitly set anything to affect it directly. It is usually derived information based on multiple sources of data that provide an insight into a user's inclinations and choices.

A good example would be serving a page that has only the content that a user is authorized to use. In this case, the portal reads the user's profile from the authentication system, runs some authorization logic, and, based on the criteria for display, generates a page. Personalization typically involves the execution of some business logic on the server side, before a page is generated. A well-designed personalized page expects and anticipates the user's wants and needs, and generates content appropriately, resulting in higher efficiency and user satisfaction.

Customization, in contrast, is an activity that a user of the portal performs to arrange or organize content in the best possible manner once it has been served. It is the ability to create a page that best fits a user's personal liking. The user sets their preferences and gets a customized page as expected. Some good examples would be the choice of colors and fonts, moving the positions of blocks of information on a page, specifying locale information such as the preferred weather zip-code, displaying various stock quotes, and so on.

Personalizing the portal

Personalizing a portal application for the user typically involves the use of the following three components of the application:

1. **Content and Information Architecture**: The organization of content on the portal that allows easy modification and tuning, for meeting the user's expectations. This relates to changing and refining content on portal pages to reflect a user's interests.

2. **User Profile**: Information about a user, including their roles and attributes, that can be effectively leveraged to filter, create role-based access, and pre-set preferences. Users can be assigned various levels of access to the portal content, and access to the content on the server can either be allowed or denied based on these access levels.

3. **Tools and Technology**: Actual implementation pieces, which include components such as filters, rules engines, and so on to tie our other two components together, and provide effective implementations of solutions. Where there are content and configuration options to personalize the content, custom application flows can be developed that explicitly provide personalized content to a user.

For example, let us consider a portal user who has pre-determined access rights to portal components. To personalize the page for this user, we first have to understand the structure of the pages and the organization of content on them. Some portlets might be okay, while others might be beyond the user's rights. Secondly, we need to inspect the user's profile and extract the information we need to make the correct decisions. In this case, we need the details of the user and their associated access rights. Finally, we can use the information about the user to create a filter, or pass it to a rule that helps to facilitate page generation, which excludes all the elements of the page that the user should not have access to, and includes the ones to which the user should have access.

Overall, personalization of portal pages in JBoss portal can be achieved in two ways:

1. Personalized user interface
2. Personalized content

A personalized user interface deals purely with the physical display of content, including backgrounds, colors, and so on. Personalized content deals with content and information on the page that is targeted for the user.

However, before we go into the details of these categories, let us briefly talk about the types of personalization models on which most actions are based.

Personalization models

There are three distinct personalization models for portal pages. These are **User Profile-based**, **Rules-based**, and **Collaborative Filtering** models. They are primarily differentiated by their content structure, user information, and the nature of the activity that needs to be performed on the server.

User profile-based

These are the types of personalization that are solely driven by the attributes, choices, preferences, security rights, and so on, of a user. Typical examples are the display of portal pages in a user's preferred language, and using their preferred colors and layout.

Rules-based

These are personalization models based on a certain set of pre-determined business rules. For example, when a user expresses interest in a certain product category and price range, the portal can execute a business rule to show all of the books in that category and price range.

Collaborative filtering

Sometimes, the content on a portal page is generated not by pre-determined business rules, but by the actions of other users or peers. User preferences, choices, and the need for a collective set of users, can dictate the content on the page for a new user who potentially belongs to a similar category. For example, when one selects a certain book, a collaborative filter can be applied to personalize the content that recommends other books purchased by users belonging to the same user group.

Personalized interface

This category of personalization involves changing the look and feel of the portal pages served to the user, based on various factors that were discussed earlier. This is not concerned with the content shown in the pages, or any visibility rules that a portlet may or may not have. A personalized interface deals purely with structural changes in the presentation of the page.

Personalization of the interface can be performed in multiple ways, depending on the extent of the changes that we want to make to each page component.

The portal server offers three components that can be configured to manage the personalization of the interface. These are as follows:

1. Layouts
2. Themes
3. RenderSets

A portal page is mostly composed of page fragments generated by portlets. The decoration and layout of these portlets is managed by the portal, to allow maximum utilization of real estate on the page. A portal can also add some additional features around portlets, such as drag-drop controls, and so on.

Layouts are used to manage the physical allocation of resources and components on the portal page, while themes are intended to manage the overall tone and color of the page, with the goal of highlighting the components of the page. Themes are a way of personalizing the visual aspects of pages, such as colors, fonts, images, and so on. Layouts are implemented using JSPs and servlets, whereas themes are implemented using CSS style sheets, JavaScript, and images.

Also, portal layouts adhere to the standards set by the portal page design. The portal page consists of regions, and within each region, there is an order. For every portlet assigned to the page, the region and the order within the region need to be specified. Hence, a portal page request involves rendering the layout, and assigning all of the portlets to specific regions within this the layout.

RenderSets are a link between a layout and a theme, and deal with rendering the markup required around a portlet that is described by the layout; combined with the theme, the page is assigned. In other words, while the portlets described by the layouts won't change in different layouts, the nature of how they are presented on a page changes based on the properties of the page theme. RenderSets perform the task of merging a portlet layout with the page theme.

In the next few sections, we will talk about Layouts, Themes, and RenderSets in more detail, including their configuration options. Later, we will use an example of a page header to demonstrate how page content can be customized to achieve personalization.

Layouts

Layouts aggregate all of the content generated by the portlet based on region and order, merge them with some additional content provided by the portal, and serve a response back to the user.

Layouts can be defined by either the portal, or the page, or both. In case layouts are defined by both the portal and the page, the page takes priority. A servlet or a JSP can implement a layout, and the portal server uses the appropriate layout based on the configuration set for the portal or page.

A layout descriptor file, `portal-layouts.xml`, contains the definition of a layout. The file is deployed as part of a normal web application. The layout deployer parses the file before registering the layouts with the layout service of the portal. A layout service is the registry of all available layouts and RenderSets.

Let us create a layout for our example portal application, MyCompany. The following is a snippet of `portal-layouts.xml` that goes into the `WEB-INF` directory of the portal application WAR file:

```
<layout>
        <name>mycompany_threecol</name>
        <uri>/layout/threecol/index.jsp</uri>
        <uri state="maximized">/layout/threecol/maximized.jsp</uri>
        <regions>
            <region name="left"/>
            <region name="center"/>
            <region name="right"/>
        </regions>
    </layout>
```

The layout file declares a new layout for the MyCompany portal and assigns an ID of mycompany_threecol to it. This is a custom layout that is composed of three columns on a page. We will use this to expand our home page from two columns to three columns. The declarations in the <uri> element in the previous code snippet refer to two different layout JSPs for two different page states. /layouts/threecol/index.jsp refers to a layout for the default state, whereas /layouts/threecol/maximized.jsp corresponds to the layout of the maximized state. The <regions> node declars the regions for the layout. Currently, we have defined three regions.

The file goes in the /WEB-INF directory, and the layout JSP references go in the application root directory.

Creating layouts

The following listing of the /layouts/threecol/index.jsp page should provide a fairly complete picture of how the layout JSP is structured. This is the JSP we will use to organize the layout of our portal home page.

```jsp
<%@ page import="org.jboss.portal.server.PortalConstants" %>
<%@page import="java.util.ResourceBundle"%>
<%@ taglib uri="/WEB-INF/theme/portal-layout.tld" prefix="p" %>
<%-- ResourceBundle rb = ResourceBundle.getBundle("Resource",
                                 request.getLocale()); --%>
<!DOCTYPE html PUBLIC "-//W3C//DTD XHTML 1.0 Transitional//EN"
"http://www.w3.org/TR/xhtml1/DTD/xhtml1-transitional.dtd">
<html xmlns="http://www.w3.org/1999/xhtml">
<head>
    <title>MyCompany Portal</title>
    <meta http-equiv="Content-Type" content="text/html;"/>
    <script type="text/javascript"></script>
    <!-- inject the theme, default to the Renewal theme if nothing
                      is selected for the portal or the page -->
    <p:theme themeName="renewal"/>
    <!-- insert header content that was possibly set by portlets
                                          on the page -->
    <p:headerContent/>
    <%@include file="common/modal_head.jsp"%>
</head>
<body id="body">
<p:region regionName='AJAXScripts' regionID='AJAXScripts'/>
<%@include file="common/modal_body.jsp"%>
<div id="portal-container">
    <div id="sizer">
        <div id="expander">
            <div id="logoName"></div>
```

```
            <table border="0" cellpadding="0" cellspacing="0"
                                id="header-container">
        <tr>
            <td align="center" valign="top" id="header">
                <!-- Utility controls -->
                <p:region regionName='dashboardnav' regionID=
                                        'dashboardnav'/>

                <!-- navigation tabs and such -->
                <p:region regionName='navigation'
                        regionID='navigation'/>
                <div id="spacer"></div>
            </td>
        </tr>
        </table>
        <div id="content-container">
            <table>
                <tr>
                    <td valign="top" width="33%">
                    <!-- insert the content of the 'left' region of the
                        page, and assign the css selector id 'regionA' -->
                    <p:region regionName='left' regionID='left'/>
                    </td>
                    <td valign="top" width="34%">
                    <!-- insert the content of the 'center' region of
                    the page, and assign the css selector id 'regionB' -->
                    <p:region regionName='center' regionID='center'/>
                    </td>
                    <td valign="top" width="33%">
                    <!-- insert the content of the 'center' region of
                    the page, and assign the css selector id 'regionC' -->
                    <p:region regionName='right' regionID='right'/>
                    </td>
                </tr>
            </table>
            <hr class="cleaner"/>
        </div>
    </div>
  </div>
  <div id="footer-container" class="portal-copyright">
  (c) MyCompany Portal<br/>
  </div>
  <p:region regionName='AJAXFooter' regionID='AJAXFooter'/>
</div>
</body>
</html>
```

This is a straightforward JSP page that segments the page into three vertical areas. These regions will be populated by portlets and content on the page. We can see that there are some special tags being used in the code. These make the code readable and also provide encapsulated functionality. The AJAX tags are to be added to the AJAX library support, which is provided by default by the JBoss server.

Using the layout JSP tags

The layout JSP can be cumbersome to create and maintain if it is developed from scratch. Hence, JBoss portal server offers a set of JSP tag libraries that can make the development of the layout JSPs much easier. The resulting code is easier to develop, read, and maintain.

There are two tag libraries that provide various features, depending on the approach for creating layouts:

1. `theme-basic-lib.tld`
2. `portal-layout.tld`

The `theme-basic-lib.tld` library assumes that the regions, portlet windows, and portlet decorations will be managed inside the JSP, whereas the `portal-layout. tld` library assumes that RenderSets will assume the responsibility of managing the regions, portlet windows, and decorations. Given that the `portal-layout` tag library doesn't have to deal with the responsibilities managed by the RenderSet, it is easier to use and enhance.

The example of layout JSP, which was shown earlier, uses the `portal-layout.tld` tag library. There are three distinct tags in the library:

1. `theme`: This allows dynamic configuration of the theme for the current request. It uses a default value if none is assigned. For example, in the above layout, we can see the reference `<p:theme themeName="renewal"/>`.

2. `headerContent`: This allows dynamic updating of header content. We used the tag `<p:headerContent/>` in the earlier layout definition.

3. `region`: Works with RenderSet to create all of the portlets for a given area and generates page fragments. It uses the `regionName` and `regionID` parameters to instruct the RenderSet to use the appropriate location on the page and the corresponding style sheet associated with it. The following tags defined the region in the layout.

   ```
   <p:region regionName='AJAXScripts' regionID='AJAXScripts'/>
   ```

   This tag is used for adding AJAX library support to the page.

Configuring layouts

Layouts can be configured declaratively and programmatically. Programmatic layout configuration involves working with a layout service, and can get fairly complicated for typical personalization needs. Hence, using declarative configuration is easier and, in most cases, is a better option for configuring and working with layouts.

The following steps are involved in configuring custom layouts for a portal or a page. As mentioned earlier, a layout can be specified at the portal level as well as at the page level. The page level specification always takes precedence.

1. Create a `portal-layout.xml` for the application and place it in the `WEB-INF/` folder of the portal application. The server will automatically detect and load the file at run time, along with some metadata. Additional layouts and, as we will see later, additional themes, can be added to run time behavior by adding new files to the folder.

2. Update the `*-object.xml` JBoss portal descriptor to tie the portal or the portal pages to the newly-created layout referenced in `portal-layout.xml`.

    The `view-object.xml`, used in our example is now edited to include references to the new layout that we created earlier. It now appears as follows:

```
<?xml version="1.0" encoding="UTF-8"?>
<deployments>
    <deployment>
        <if-exists>overwrite</if-exists>
        <parent-ref/>
        <portal>
          <portal-name>mycompany</portal-name>

          <page>
             <page-name>default</page-name>
               <window>
             <window-name>ViewPortletWindow</window-name>
             <instance-ref>ViewPortletInstance</instance-ref>
                     <region>right</region>
                     <height>1</height>
               </window>
            <properties>
               <property>
                  <name>layout.id</name>
                    <value>mycompany_threecol</value>
               </property>
            </properties>
          </page>
          <page>
```

```
            <page-name>Tools</page-name>
        </page>
      </portal>
    </deployment>
  </deployments>
```

The `layout.id` property is set with the value of a layout called `mycompany_threecol`, which is defined in the `portal-layouts.xml` file. As you can see from the configuration file, we have the custom layout set for the **default** page to allow us the option to configure a different layout for each page of our application.

Layouts can also be specified at the portal level, but the page layout takes preference. From a personalization perspective, such granular control offers applications the flexibility to assign layouts to certain pages that are best oriented towards the functions of a certain set of users. In other words, specific pages can now be "personalized" and served.

3. Copy the files `portal-layouts.xml` and `*-object.xml` to the `WEB-INF/` folder of the application.

Once deployed, the portal server can then pick the files from the folder and add them to the run time for the application, so that it can start using the new layout.

Before we see what the view looks like with the new layout, let us also tweak a few more related aspects called *Themes* and *RenderSets*.

Themes

A theme is another important component for personalization, which relates to visual aspects of a page such as fonts, colors, images, and so on. A theme is predominantly a combination of CSS style sheets, JavaScript files, and images. Themes work in collaboration with layouts and RenderSets to create the visual elements of a page when the page response is sent back to the browser client. We will talk more about RenderSets in the next section, but for now, it is sufficient to know that they are a mechanism to generate markup around a portlet. Unlike layouts and RenderSets, creating and manipulating themes doesn't involve any binaries, which makes them easier to create and deploy. Themes, if used appropriately, can achieve the same, or better, results than one would get by changing layouts or RenderSets, and without the added complexity. Due to the simple nature of the markup, theme developers can work within the knowledge of HTML, multi-media, and JavaScript, without having to learn JSP or similar methods. Themes can also be deployed during runtime and on separate web applications as a part of static content, as there are no executables involved, and the content is largely referenced through plain HTML.

Defining themes

Just as with layouts, themes are defined in a descriptor file called `portal-themes.xml`, which is located in the `WEB-INF/` folder of the portal application. Also, similar to layouts, the theme deployer scans the descriptor file and adds the themes to the `ThemeService`. `ThemeService` is a registry of all of the available themes within the portal.

Let's create a new theme for our application and define it in `portal-themes.xml`, the theme descriptor.

```
<?xml version="1.0" encoding="UTF-8"?>
<themes>
   <theme>
      <name>mycompany_theme</name>
      <link rel="stylesheet" id="main_css" href="/theme/
         portal_style.css" type="text/css"/>
   </theme>
</themes>
```

As we can see in the preceding example, there is a name assigned to the theme called `mycompany_theme`, and an associated CSS. The CSS file has to be created and placed in the appropriate directory. We have used the CSS file to customize the logs, fonts, colors, and so on, to our specific needs.

The `portal-themes` descriptor file can also be used to include limited HTML and JavaScript code.

Although for our example we have created only a single theme, it is not uncommon to see multiple themes for a single application, to address specific page content on the portal.

Configuring themes

We saw how the layout is defined, in an earlier section of this chapter. Themes are defined in the same manner as the portal descriptors. Themes can again be defined at the portal level or at the page level, but page always takes precedence over portal. In addition, themes can also be defined within the layout as a JSP tag.

```
<p:theme themeName="mycompany_theme" />
```

As shown in the following example, we have now associated our default page with the `mycompany_theme` we have just created:

```
<?xml version="1.0" encoding="UTF-8"?>
<deployments>
   <deployment>
```

```
<if-exists>overwrite</if-exists>
<parent-ref/>
 <portal>
    <portal-name>mycompany</portal-name>

 <page>
        <page-name>default</page-name>
     <window>
            <window-name>ViewPortletWindow</window-name>
            <instance-ref>ViewPortletInstance</instance-ref>
            <region>right</region>
            <height>1</height>
     </window>
      <properties>
      <property>
        <name>layout.id</name>
         <value>mycompany_threecol</value>
      </property>
      <property>
        <name>theme.id</name>
        <value>mycompany_theme</value>
      </property>
      </properties>
     </page>
     <page>
            <page-name>Tools</page-name>
     </page>
    </portal>
   </deployment>
  </deployments>
```

Similarly, themes are used when layouts are created using the JSP tag library. The
following snippet illustrates theme declaration as a JSP tag:

```
<%@ page import="org.jboss.portal.server.PortalConstants" %>
<%@page import="java.util.ResourceBundle"%>
<%@ taglib uri="/WEB-INF/theme/portal-layout.tld" prefix="p" %>
<% ResourceBundle rb = ResourceBundle.getBundle("Resource", request.
getLocale()); %>
<!DOCTYPE html PUBLIC "-//W3C//DTD XHTML 1.0 Transitional//EN"
"http://www.w3.org/TR/xhtml1/DTD/xhtml1-transitional.dtd">
<html xmlns="http://www.w3.org/1999/xhtml">
<head>
    <title>MyCompany Portal</title>
    <meta http-equiv="Content-Type" content="text/html;"/>
```

```
    <script type="text/javascript"></script>
    <!-- inject the theme, default to the Renewal theme if nothing is
    selected for the portal or the page -->
    <p:theme themeName="renewal"/>
    <!-- insert header content that was possibly set by portlets on
    the page -->
    <p:headerContent/>
    <%@include file="/layouts/common/modal_head.jsp"%>
</head>
```

In the `<head>` tag, the `themeName` is defined as `renewal`. In our case, this theme will be used only if our declared theme cannot be used for some reason.

Similar to layouts and RenderSets, themes can also be effectively used to control granular page-level personalization of portal components such as portal pages and portlets. But the ease of development and deployment makes themes an exciting choice for personalizing the interface of a pre-determined set of pages that are to be served to the users.

RenderSets

A RenderSet is a link between the layout and a page theme. It is used to generate the markup around portlets and portlet regions. Although the markup remains the same for all portlet windows, there are major changes in colors, fonts, images, and so on, for each portlet that is displayed. A layout passes information about the region, which the RenderSet maps to the associated theme, and generates the markup around regions and portlets, which are used by the CSS theme to generate the final appearance.

Using RenderSets

Render interfaces are specified in the `org.jboss.portal.theme.render` package, and correspond to each of the four markup container on a portal page.

The four markup containers and their interfaces are as follows:

1. `Region`: Arranges the positions and order of each portlet window. Its corresponding interface is `RegionRenderer`.

2. `Window`: Is responsible for activities related to a portlet window, such as the portlet title. Its corresponding interface is `WindowRenderer`.

3. `Decoration`: Is responsible for assigning the correct decoration to the portlet, based on the portlet modes and window states available to the portlet. Its corresponding interface is `DecorationRenderer`.

4. `PortletContent`: This is the markup produced by the portlet itself. Its corresponding interface is `PortletRenderer`.

The interesting aspect of RenderSets, from a personalization perspective, is the way we can tailor the markup and visual display of a page to the user's needs by adapting the RenderSets.

As with to layouts, RenderSets can be applied at the portal level or at the individual page level. Let's add a reference to a RenderSet for our example. We will call it `mycompany_renderer`. Again, we use the same portal descriptor, `view-object.xml`, but now we will provide a reference to the `theme.renderSetId` property with the assigned renderer.

```xml
<?xml version="1.0" encoding="UTF-8"?>
<deployments>
   <deployment>
      <if-exists>overwrite</if-exists>
      <parent-ref/>
       <portal>
         <portal-name>mycompany</portal-name>

      <page>
            <page-name>default</page-name>
         <window>
               <window-name>ViewPortletWindow</window-name>
               <instance-ref>ViewPortletInstance</instance-ref>
               <region>right</region>
               <height>1</height>
         </window>
          <properties>
          <property>
            <name>layout.id</name>
              <value>mycompany_threecol</value>
          </property>
          <property>
            <name>theme.id</name>
            <value>mycompany_theme</value>
          </property>
          <property>
            <name>theme.renderSetId</name>
            <value>mycompany_divRenderer</value>
          </property>
          </properties>
         </page>
         <page>
               <page-name>Tools</page-name>
         </page>
```

```
        </portal>
      </deployment>
    </deployments>
```

We are invoking our custom renderer called `mycompany_renderer`.

Just as with layouts, page-level configuration takes precedence over portal-level configuration.

The RenderSet's values are declared in their own file, called `portal-renderSet.xml`, which is either saved in the `WEB-INF`/layout folder, or added to the class path.

The following is a snippet of the declaration in the `portal-renderSet.xml` file. Please note that we are using the same custom name—`mycompany_renderer`. We will also be using an existing `renderer` class instead of creating a custom one, because the ones that come with the portal are exhaustive enough to cover most portal application requirements.

```
<portal-renderSet>
  <renderSet name="mycompany_divRenderer">
    <set content-type="text/html">
      <ajax-enabled>true</ajax-enabled>
      <region-renderer>
        org.jboss.portal.theme.impl.render.div.DivRegionRenderer
      </region-renderer>
      <window-renderer>
        org.jboss.portal.theme.impl.render.div.DivWindowRenderer
      </window-renderer>
      <portlet-renderer>
        org.jboss.portal.theme.impl.render.div.DivPortletRenderer
      </portlet-renderer>
      <decoration-renderer>
        org.jboss.portal.theme.impl.render.div.DivDecorationRenderer
      </decoration-renderer>
    </set>
  </renderSet>
</portal-renderSet>
```

By adjusting the combination of RenderSets and the corresponding renderers, we can create a pre-determined set of portal pages and portlets that are personalized for a user who uses these pages.

With the configuration now in place, let's build and deploy our application. As we have created a three-column page, for consistency, let's add a simple portlet to the center column.

Once the application has been deployed, the **Admin** console shows the following, indicating that the portlet has been deployed, as described by the descriptor. The **ContentPortlet** is deployed in the center region of the layout.

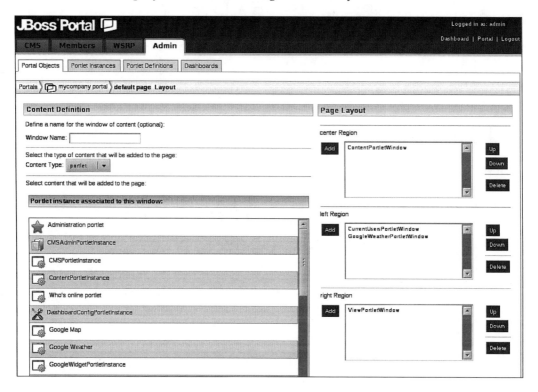

Let's now go to the default page theme setting and confirm that the layout, theme, and renderer are there, as we declared.

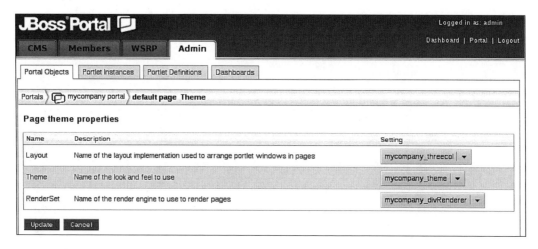

As we can see from the preceding screenshot, all of the settings are using our custom components.

Finally, let's log in as a user and verify our default home page.

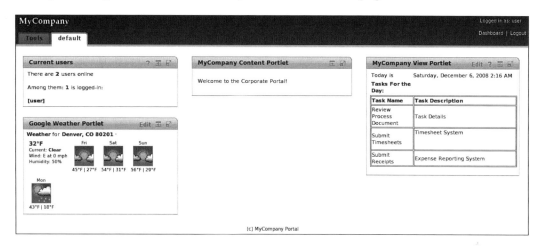

This screenshot shows a custom implementation of our page. It is a three-column page with a customized logo and footer, as prescribed by the layout, theme, and RenderSet. Also, notice that the new portlet now populates the central column.

All of the configurations related to layouts, themes, and RenderSets can also be performed from the **Admin** console. The application can deploy new layouts, themes, and RenderSets, which can be then fairly easily configured, at the required level of granularity (portal or page), using the **Admin** console.

A good example for understanding personalized user interface is the page header. In the following example, we will see how the header uses the theme and the layout.

Custom development

Custom development is an option that can be used when the pure configuration of layouts, themes, and RenderSets is not sufficient for user interface changes. In such cases, it might be useful to manually edit the template files and add code to build a customized interface.

The portal header is one such place. Let us look deeper into the personalization of headers.

The header consists of two regions. The first region deals with the navigation links, and the other deals with the navigation tabs. It is now a matter of changing the presentation of either or both of these regions. There are a couple of ways of changing the header:

- **Change the theme CSS**: This can be used to alter the look and feel of the header—that is, colors, fonts, tab structure, and so on. Changes to CSS cannot be used to change *content* in the header.

- **Modify the** `header.jsp` **and** `tabs.jsp` **files assigned to the header layout**: If there is a need for significant flexibility, changing the source files, `header.jsp` and `tabs.jsp`, might be a better option. The source can be changed to add, edit, or remove any content on the page, including the CSS files.

Modifying header.jsp

The `header.jsp` and `tabs.jsp` files can be found in the directory, `jboss-portal.sar\portal-core.war\WEB-INF\jsp\header`.

`header.jsp` content generates the links on the top right of the default theme. `tabs.jsp` generates the page tabs on the left.

We can either update the files directly, or better, create a new set of JSP files and change the current pointer to point to our new files. This can be done by editing the file: `jboss-portal.sar/META-INF/jboss-service.xml`.

The following snippet from this file highlights the references to `header.jsp` and `tabs.jsp`.

```
<mbean code="org.jboss.portal.core.aspects.controller.
            PageCustomizerInterceptor"
       name="portal:service=Interceptor,
                type=Command,
                name=PageCustomizer"
       xmbean-dd=""
       xmbean-code="org.jboss.portal.jems.as.system.
                JBossServiceModelMBean">
<xmbean/>
<attribute name="TargetContextPath">/portal-core</attribute>
<attribute name="HeaderPath">
    /WEB-INF/jsp/header/header.jsp
```

```
</attribute>
<attribute name="TabsPath">
   /WEB-INF/jsp/header/tabs.jsp
</attribute>
<!-- Overrides the value of core.login.namespace in config.xml  -->
<!--  attribute name="LoginNamespace">dashboard</attribute -->
<depends optional-attribute-name="Config" proxy-type="attribute">
    portal:service=ServerConfig
</depends>
</mbean>
```

The description of the preceding snippet is as follows:

1. `TargetContextPath`: Describes the reference web application

2. `HeaderPath`: Points to the location of `header.jsp` with reference to the above mentioned `TargetContextPath`

3. `TabsPath`: Points to the location of the `tabs.jsp` file, with reference to the web application path mentioned earlier

Creating new JSPs

One of the advantages of writing our own JSPs is the choice we have of injecting added information to make our pages richer. A few of the attributes that are available and can be used are as follows:

- `org.jboss.portal.header.USER:`
- `org.jboss.portal.header.LOGIN_URL:URL`
- `org.jboss.portal.header.DASHBOARD_URL`
- `org.jboss.portal.header.DEFAULT_PORTAL_URL`
- `org.jboss.portal.header.SIGN_OUT_URL:URL`

For example, let's say we want to create a personalized header for our portal that uses the user's preferred name, adds today's date and time, and mentions the ID used. The preferred name is something we have asked the user to set in their profile, and we have pre-populated the server preferences with this information.

The following code snippet from the `header.jsp` file should take care of the custom header:

```
<%@ page import="org.jboss.portal.identity.User" %>
   <%@ page import="java.util.Date" %>
   <%@ page import="java.text.DateFormat" %>
   <%@ page import="java.util.Locale" %>

<%
```

```
User user = (User) renderRequest.getAttribute("org.jboss.portal.
header.USER");
    DateFormat df = DateFormat.getDateTimeInstance(DateFormat.FULL,
                    DateFormat.SHORT, Locale.getDefault());
  %>
   <p> Portal Account For: <%= renderRequest.getPreferences()
                    .getValue("preferredName","Not selected") %>
   Today is : <%=df.format(new Date())%> <br>
   <% if (user != null) { %>
        You are logged in as : <%= user.getUserName() %>
   <% } %>
```

Modifying tabs.jsp

Similar to header.jsp, the existing tabs.jsp page can be updated, or a new one created with reference to jboss-service.xml.

The following two request attributes are provided by portals, and are used to generate the navigation tabs and their links:

- org.jboss.portal.api.PORTAL_NODE: Provides access to the portal node from which peer and child nodes can be listed. The tabs we currently see in the default implementation use this attribute.

- org.jboss.portal.api.PORTAL_RUNTIME_CONTEXT: Whereas the PORTAL_NODE attribute provides the node definition, this attribute provides the URL links to the nodes. Again, the tabs we see by default use this attribute to add links to each page.

The above attributes can be used to provide features such as a breadcrumb trail, and so on, on each page for better usability.

Personalized content

Up to now, we have been discussing how screen elements such as windows, pages, portlets, and so on, can be organized effectively to personalize the user interface. We have not yet discussed anything about personalizing the content that is served in these pages, portlets, and windows. Although the layout is important, the personalization of content plays a bigger role in creating a tailored environment for a user. Personalized content is relevant, concise, easily accessible, and informative. In this section, we will specifically discuss how to generate content that is built around a user.

Personalization of portal page content is broadly based on three sets of data available to the portal server.

1. A user's security and profile information
2. A user's chosen set of preferences
3. Any analytic insights observed through browsing patterns and other avenues

Let's understand the personalized portlet generation based on each one of these, in detail.

Access-level based portlets

A user's profile can have a significant role in determining a portlet's visibility and its content. Access rights can determine whether the user is even allowed to see or use the portlet, whereas, a user's attributes might provide an opportunity to create content that best suits the user's position, qualification, or clearance.

To personalize a portlet based on user attributes, we have to perform the following actions:

*   **Define the User Attributes**: User attribute names are defined in the portal deployment descriptor. These names are later used by the portlet and the API to retrieve user information. The following code lists the deployment descriptor entry for user attributes:

```
<portlet-app>
        <user-attribute>
           <description>User First Name</description>
           <name>user.name.first</name>
        </user-attribute>
        <user-attribute>
           <description>User Last Name</description>
           <name>user.name.last</name>
        </user-attribute>
        <user-attribute>
           <description>User eMail</description>
           <name>user.email</name>
        </user-attribute>
        <user-attribute>
           <description>Company </description>
           <name>user.organization</name>
        </user-attribute>
    <portlet-app>
```

- **Map the User Attribute to Values**: This is done using a mapping file named `profile-config.xml`. The following entry illustrates the mapping of one attribute:

```
<profile>
      <property>
         <name>user.name.first</name>
         <type>java.lang.String</type>
         <access-mode>read-only</access-mode>
         <usage>mandatory</usage>
         <display-name xml:lang="en">Name</display-name>
         <description xml:lang="en">
             The user's first name
         </description>
         <mapping>
            <database>
                <type>column</type>
                <value>user_fname</value>
            </database>
         </mapping>
      </property>
</profile>
```

- **Access the User Attributes**: Request attributes offer a non-modifiable `Map` object containing the user attributes for a user associated with the current request. The user attribute `Map` can be obtained from the `PortletRequest` interface's `USER_INFO` constant. Obviously, this assumes that the user has been authenticated. The following sample snippet of code illustrates the retrieval of user attributes:

```
   . . .
Map userAttr = (Map) request.getAttribute(PortletRequest.USER_INFO);
String firstName = (userAttr!=null) ? (String)
                   userAttr.get("user.name.first") : "";
String lastName = (userAttr!=null) ? (String)
                   userAttr.get("user.name.last") : "";
   . . .
```

Preference-based portlets

Whereas access-level and user attributes are relatively static pieces of information usually gathered from sources other than the user, preferences-based portlets are generated using a combination of preferences set explicitly by the user and derivative information based on the user's preferences.

Let us take an example of a user who sets a language preference. Generating content in the language of choice is an aspect of customization, and we will briefly talk about the process of internationalization in the next section. However, a preference-based portlet will not only consider this preference, but will also correlate other aspects to the preference. In our case, a travel portal can consider the language preference and customize the news or weather for the given region.

In the next section on customization, we will see how these preferences are set. But here, generating preference-based portlets is largely a programmatic implementation that leverages the `PortletPreferences` API, combined with rules on the server side that generate the content.

Analytics-based portlets

As a portal grows in size in terms of the number of users, we begin to start seeing trends in user behavior and user experiences based on the data we accumulate. This data can be mined to generate predictive information on what content is relevant for the user. An important aspect to note here is that the content is not created or generated for a particular user, but for a set of users who exhibit certain common behaviors and attributes.

A good example is the recommendation of books and corresponding references on a book retail portal, based on the category of books that a user has been browsing lately.

Again, such an implementation requires some pre-work in running analytics on the data gathered from server logs, user experience logs, and some business intelligence indicators. The trends are then matched against the portal user-base before the content is finally created.

Customizing the portal

As discussed at the beginning of this chapter, customization is another important way of delivering the application in a way that is preferred by the user. However, unlike personalization, customization is initiated by a user for convenience, expediency, and usability. Sometimes, customization settings are temporary for a given session.

There are many ways to customize portal pages, portlets, and content. The salient ones are setting preferences, drag-drop component repositioning, and changing the physical attributes of a page, such as font sizes, colors, and so on.

Setting preferences

Preferences allow the user of a portal to save information about a personal set of choices so that the portal output is customized for them every time they interact with the portal. Customization can either be in behavior, or in the output. An example of customized behavior is using Google Finance for retrieving stock information. An example of output customization is the number of FAQs displayed on a single page for a given topic.

The portlet specification provides options for setting preferences on the server. These can be overridden by the user. Let us take out example MyCompany portal application, and add some default preferences to the ContentPortlet. The following snippet of code from the portlet.xml portal deployment descriptor illustrates the setting of default preferences on the server. When the portlet is first deployed, or in scenarios when there is no user currently logged on, preferences are set by adding a new <portlet-preferences> section for each portlet definition.

```
<portlet>
    <portlet-name>ContentPortlet</portlet-name>
    <portlet-class>
        org.mycompany.portlet.content.ContentPortlet
    </portlet-class>
    <supports>
        <mime-type>text/html</mime-type>
        <portlet-mode>VIEW</portlet-mode>
    </supports>
    <portlet-info>
        <title>MyCompany Content Portlet</title>
        </portlet-info>
    <! -- Portlet Preferences -->
    <portlet-preferences>
    <!-- Output Preference -->
        <preference>
            <name>color</name>
            <value>Magenta</value>
        </preference>
        <preference>
            <name>shape</name>
            <value>Spiral</value>
        </preference>
        <preference>
            <name>size</name>
            <value>large</value>
            <read-only>true</read-only>
        </preference>
    </portlet-preferences>
</portlet>
```

The rights to update and overwrite preferences are managed through personalization policies defined on the server. The portlet has three preferences that are defined, along with their default values. In the example above, we can also see a preference with the tag `<read-only>true</read-only>`. This indicates that the preference cannot be changed and it is only for reading. For editable preferences, portlets can change the value preference attributes by using the `setValue`, `setValues`, and `reset` methods of the `PortletPreferences` interface.

The `ContentPortlet` will provide a default set of preferences, and we will then allow the user to personalize the page by defining a new set of preferences.

Now that we have the default values defined, let's edit the `portlet` class to allow the setting of preferences by the user. The `PortalPreferences` class is responsible for storing and retrieving preference information. However, all invocations to `PortalPreferences` should only be in the `processAction` method.

Hence, our new `processAction` method looks like this:

```
public void processAction (ActionRequest request, ActionResponse
    actionResponse)
  throws PortletException, java.io.IOException {
      PortletPreferences pref = request.getPreferences();
      pref.setValue("color",request.getParameter("color"));
      pref.setValue("shape",request.getParameter("shape"));
      pref.store();
  actionResponse.setPortletMode(PortletMode.VIEW);
  actionResponse.setRenderParameters(request.getParameterMap());
  }
```

The rest of the methods remain the same. Once deployed, the application now shows the default preferences when there is either no user logged in, or the user has not selected any preference.

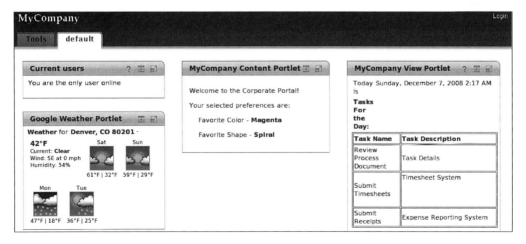

The user can then edit their preferences, which will be saved in their portal preference data.

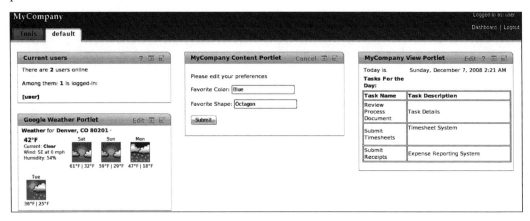

The next time the user loads the page, it will be customized with the values that the user has defined. These values are retained even after the user logs off and logs back in again.

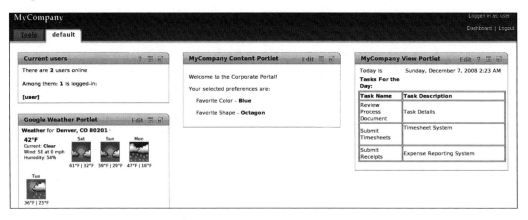

Although this example is very simple, it is meant to explain a very important aspect of the portal server. Because the server retains user choices and preferences between multiple sessions, we can develop portal applications that look up these preference values and customize the page accordingly. It is also important to note that the portal server has managed all of the details of capturing, retaining, and co-relating the preference information, without the developer having to deal with databases and code.

Internationalization and localization

Internationalization (I18N) and **Localization (L10N)** are fairly common requirements in portals. They are primarily used to customize content as per the locale and language specified in the user's preferences. They can also be used to customize number, date and time formats, and to provide messages in the user's preferred language.

The portlet deployment descriptor allows for localization at deploy and run times. The deploy time values are the ones that are used when a given portlet is deployed. The runtime option is the definition of a set of supported localized language alternatives.

In the deployment descriptor, the default value is English, en, although more languages can also be declared. The following example illustrates the deploy and runtime declaration of locales:

```
<portlet-app>
    <description xml:lang="en">
        Portlet displaying the time in different time zones
    </description>
    <description xml:lang="de">
        Dieses Portlet zeigt die Zeit in verschiedenen Zeitzonen an.
    </description>
    <portlet-name>TimeZoneClock</portlet-name>
    <display-name xml:lang="en">
        Time Zone Clock Portlet
    </display-name>
    <display-name xml:lang="de">
        ZeitzonenPortlet
    </display-name>
    <portlet-class>
        com.myco.samplets.util.zoneclock.ZoneClock
    </portlet-class>
    <expiration-cache>60</expiration-cache>
    <supports>
        <mime-type>text/html</mime-type>
        <portlet-mode>config</portlet-mode>
        <portlet-mode>edit</portlet-mode>
        <portlet-mode>help</portlet-mode>
    </supports>
    <supported-locale>en</supported-locale>
    <supported-locale>fr</supported-locale>
</portlet-app>
```

The <supported-locale> tag lists the available run-time customization options for locale.

Drag-and-drop content

This is a feature that allows users to drag-and-drop various portlet windows within a page. The option is set as a configurable parameter on the server. Once set, the user will have options available on the screen to perform dynamic and rich user interface functions such as dragging windows, repositioning portlets on a page, and so on. However, this feature is most applicable on pages that have multiple windows. There is not much use for dynamic repositioning of windows on pages that have a very small set of information blocks and only have a lot of empty space to move around. As a dashboard typically consists of multiple windows that fill the page, feature is only available on a dashboard.

The following is a brief snippet of code that sets the flag that will allow the drag-and-drop of portlet windows:

```
<deployment>
        <parent-ref />
        <if-exists>keep</if-exists>
        <context>
            <context-name>dashboard</context-name>
            <properties>
                ...
                <property>
                    <name>theme.dyna.dnd_enabled</name>
                    <value>true</value>
                </property>
                ...
            </properties>
            ...
        </context>
</deployment>
```

By setting the value of the parameter `theme.dyna.dnd_enabled` to `true`, we have now set the dashboard page to have drag-and-drop features. The user can now customize the screen by dragging and dropping elements within the page.

Usability settings

Usability settings include using portlets for temporary functions, manipulating the state of the portlets for transient use during the session, and so on.

For example, some users like to use a portlet, such as a stock quote portlet, to get the values that are used only during their current session. They don't care about saving them. Similarly, somebody might decide to minimize or close some portlets and create more room on the page to better facilitate the task they are there for. The portal server supports features like these through its window renderers, and allows a user to configure a page that best fits their needs.

The transient information is managed by the portal using the `PortletSession` interface.

The following is a small snippet of code that illustrates how information is added to and retrieved from the portal session. These sessions are tied to the users and the browsers that they are using. As soon as the user logs out, or closes the browser, the session expires, and so does all of the data that we stored in it during the user's interaction with the portal.

```
public void processAction(ActionRequest request, ActionResponse
        response)
throws PortletException, IOException
{
...
    if (request.equals("appendPlaylist"))
    {
        PortletSession pSession = request.getPortletSession();
        PlaylList list = (PortletSession)session.
                        getAttribute("playlist");
        list.addSong(song);
        // We need to now add the updated playlist to the session
        session.setAttribute("playlist", list);
    }
...
}
```

In our example, the user temporarily wanted the convenience of picking all of the songs he or she wanted to hear during that visit. The portlet was asked to add a song to the playlist. We retrieved the current playlist from the session, added the new song, and updated the session with the new playlist.

Summary

In this chapter, we reviewed how the power of portals can be extended by facilitating features such as customization and personalization. JBoss portal provides strong features that allow a user to customize the behavior of the screen to an individual's comfort level. At the same time, it offers a vast array of options from Layouts, RenderSets, Themes, and a strong API which can anticipate a user's needs and choices, to offer personalized pages. We further extended our example portal to include custom layouts, themes and other personalization features. We also saw how we can personalize a page and offer users options to control the contents of the page.

Although personalization and customization are important, a dynamic user interface with rich features allows better usability and a richer feature set. In the next chapter, we will start looking at rich user interfaces.

6
Portals and AJAX

Dynamic, attractive, and rich interfaces have always helped in creating compelling web applications. However, in recent years, the popularity and support for asynchronous browser-to-server communication, combined with the strong client-side capabilities of JavaScript and XML, have resulted in exciting user interfaces with unprecedented functionality. **AJAX (Asynchronous JavaScript and XML)**, as the rich user interface design is commonly called, has gained wide acceptability in traditional web applications, and portals are no exception to this.

JBoss portal blends the dynamism and rich functionality offered by AJAX with its strong portal architecture to provide users with choices for developing highly-functional portal applications. The latest portlet specification, JSR-286, provides an easy and intuitive approach to implementing asynchronous calls that was not possible in JSR-168. In this chapter, we will also discuss the limitations of the current specification and walk through an example portlet to understand how AJAX can enhance portlets.

Rich user interfaces and AJAX

Rich user interfaces can be achieved by using a combination of dynamic HTML elements such as HTML and JavaScript. However, the scope of such an interface is limited to client-side behavior and has minimal functional implications due to the lack of server-side interactions. The power of **AJAX** is in its capability to provide even richer interface by supplementing its dynamic user interface with powerful functionality through seamless server-side invocation power. AJAX allows individual user interface components to communicate with the server and exchange data without the need for refreshing the whole screen. This is achieved using a process called **Web Remoting**. Web remoting, or the process of communicating between a browser and a server, can be performed in multiple ways. The popular approaches that are supported by today's browsers are **IFrames** and **XMLHttpRequest**. Dynamic HTML can be complemented with either of these methods to generate AJAX functionality.

Asynchronous JavaScript and XML or AJAX

Asynchronous communication between the client and the server forms the backbone of AJAX. Although an asynchronous request-response method can provide significant value in the development of rich functionality by itself, the results are lot more pronounced when used in conjunction with other functional standards such as CSS, DOM, JavaScript, and so on. The predominant popularity of AJAX stems from such usage.

Client-server communication can be achieved either by using IFrames, or by using the supported JavaScript function call `XMLHttpRequest()`. Due to certain limitations of IFrames, XMLHttpRequest has gained a lot more acceptance. While IFrame can also be an effective option for implementing AJAX-based solutions, in this chapter, we will focus largely on an XMLHttpRequest-based implementation. The primary advantage of using AJAX-based interfaces is that the update of content occurs without page refreshes. A typical AJAX implementation using XMLHttpRequest happens as described in the following steps:

1. An action on the client side, whether this is a mouse click or a timed refresh, triggers a client event

2. An XMLHttpRequest object is created and configured

3. The XMLHttpRequest object makes a call

4. The request is processed by a server-side component

5. The component returns an XML (or an equivalent) document containing the result

6. The XMLHttpRequest object calls the `callback()` function and processes the result

7. The HTML DOM is updated with any resulting values

The following simplified image illustrates the high-level steps involved in an AJAX request flow. The portal client page gets served to the client browser, where the execution of JavaScript functions takes place.

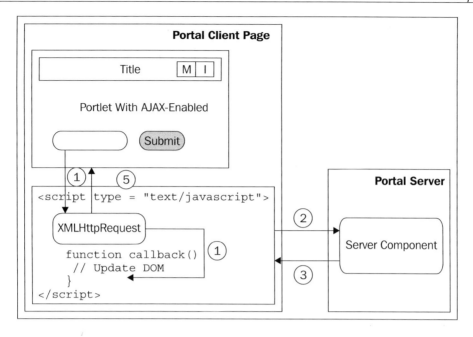

The following example illustrates the initialization of the request object and its basic use:

```
if (window.XMLHttpRequest) // Object of the current window {
    // for non-IE browsers
    request = new XMLHttpRequest();
}
else if (window.ActiveXObject){
    // For IE
    request = new ActiveXObject("Microsoft.XMLHTTP");
}
request.onreadystatechange = function()
{
    // do something to process response
};
if (request.readyState == 4){
    // everything received, OK. Do something now..
} else {
    // wait for the response to come to ready state
}
```

In subsequent sections, we will modify our sample portal application by adding AJAX functionality to one of the portlets.

AJAX in JBoss portal

AJAX has gained tremendous popularity in the traditional web application development world due to the richness and agility that it brings to user interfaces. Portals, such as JBoss portal, can also gain significantly from AJAX, in terms of implementation of both behavior and functionality.

Refreshing the page content tends to be a time-consuming and resource-intensive process. Every request that a user makes to the server, either by clicking on submissions or links, results in the portal calling doView() and a series of methods for each portlet on the page, one at a time, before aggregating the results and sending the response back to the browser. Using AJAX allows for simultaneous submissions of request in their own independent threads of execution, resulting in an asynchronous and parallel execution. The portal page refresh overhead is now only as long as the time consumed by the slowest portlet.

The response times observed by the user improve dramatically, while at the same time allowing more functionality on pages. Architecturally, vertical independent stacks of execution facilitate cleaner and more modular designs and implementations.

AJAX can be implemented in JBoss portal in the following two ways:

1. Using in-built support for asynchronous portal behavior by using configurations.
2. Writing custom behavior in portlets and page content by using AJAX libraries.

The in-built support for asynchronous behavior comprises of support for both markup and content. The markup support is in layouts and renderers, while the content is supported through configurable drag-drop and partial page refresh behavior. Almost all of the AJAX behavior supported by JBoss portal relates to asynchronous communication between the client and the portal servers. The only exception is the drag-drop behavior, which is largely view functionality.

As far as the custom development within a portlet is concerned, the options are innumerable. A portlet can be developed using many advanced frameworks that are available as either commercial or open source products. For example, user interface features such as drag-and-drops, grids, accordion selects, pull-down menus, content refresh, and so on can be implemented by using third-party libraries including Scriptaculous, JQuery, and DOJO, which have gained a strong following among developers, even on traditional applications and non-portal platforms.

In the next few sections, we will walk through an example of AJAX-enabled portlets using one of these libraries, developed on the JBoss portal platform. However, before we go into the implementation, let's step back and understand the limitations that the current portlet specification– JSR-286–addresses, facilitating easy development of AJAX portlets.

JSR-168 AJAX limitations

Before we look at the features and options provided by the new specification, let's look at how traditional JSR-168 portlets functioned. As shown in the following figure, the "Action" request invoked the `processAction` method on the server, which implemented controller logic to route it to the correct view. The "Render" request then invokes the `render` method to serve the content page to the browser.

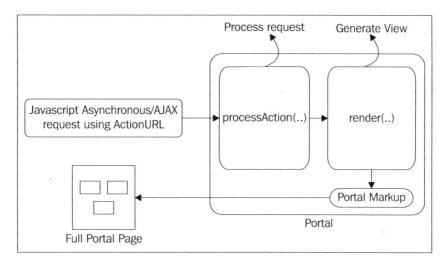

However, when the portlet uses AJAX and needs to makes an asynchronous call, it has to use `ActionURL`. This in turn follows the standard processing when `processAction` processes the request and the `render` method creates the user interface. However, now when the user interface is sent back, the portal injects some other markup and recreates the entire portal page. Hence, instead of refreshing a snippet of user interface, we end up refreshing the whole page.

The issues with JSR-168 and AJAX can be broadly summarized as follows:

- `ActionURL` and `RenderURL` point to a portal, and not to a portlet. When we point to a portal, the result is a complete portal page, even if the portlet generates only a snippet.

- As per the specification, the user interface rendered by the portlet is supposed to be aggregated with some other markup and served back to the browser. When more than only the necessary data and markup is sent back, the JavaScript code on the client side that makes the asynchronous call cannot process the request.

- Asynchronous calls are made through XMLHttpRequest, which is designed to consume and process the complete response from the portlet. With the portal processing the request in between, XMLHttpRequest cannot consume the original response for processing.

This defeats the purpose and value of using asynchronous calls to the server, and we end up with traditional full page refreshes.

There were obviously a few workarounds to this. The most common practice was to serve the request from outside of the portal container into the web container. The idea is that the AJAX call can still be made to `ActionURL`, but the `render` function copies or shares its context with a traditional Java servlet in the web container of the application server. The AJAX call can now make a direct request to the servlet and get an asynchronous response from the servlet with no interference from the portal.

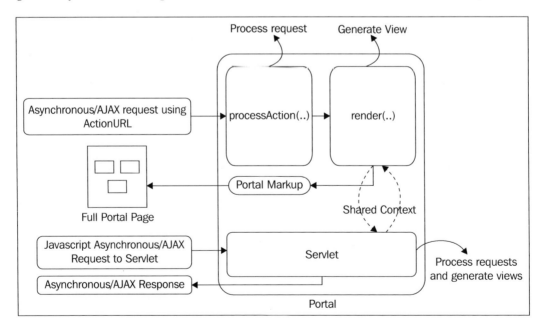

However, this is, at best, a temporary solution with limited options. Shared contexts and sessions can be invalid or stale, and it is not always possible to expose the servlets from the web container.

There was a need for a better solution, and one that was incorporated as part of the specification. JSR-286, the latest portlet specification, addresses these problems.

JSR-286 and AJAX

Among the set of features that the new portlet specification JSR-286 introduces to make things easier for AJAX implementations, are the options to directly communicate with the portlet through shared render parameters and resource serving.

Referring back to the workaround option in JSR-168, the new specification provides a standard for setting and receiving render parameters, and we no longer have to deal with manual copying OF context and parameters.

To set the `render` parameter directly to the response, all we have to do is this:

```
public class AssetPortlet extends GenericPortlet {
    public void processAction(ActionRequest request,
                        ActionResponse response) {
            response.setRenderParameter("rate", "4.5");
    }
    ...
}
```

To receive render parameters in the portlet directly from the view, we can say:

```
public class AssetPortlet extends GenericPortlet {
    public void render(RenderRequest request, RenderResponse response)
    {
            String rate = request.getParameter("rate");
            ...
    }
    ...
}
```

Similarly, the resource servicing option allows us to directly invoke the portlet from the portlet user interface, as follows:

```
ResourceURL resourceURL = renderResponse.createResourceURL()
<form action="<%= resourceURL %> method="POST">
  ...
</form>
```

Using `ResourceURL` invokes a new life cycle method called `serveResource()` on the server, as follows:

```
public void serveResource(ResourceRequest req, ResourceResponse resp)
throws PortletException, IOException
   {
       resp.setContentType("text/html");
       PrintWriter writer = resp.getWriter();

       writer.print("<p> <b>Response Markup </b>");
       writer.close();
   }
```

So, now when we use `ResourceURL` instead of `ActionURL`, the implementation of the asynchronous requests appears as follows:

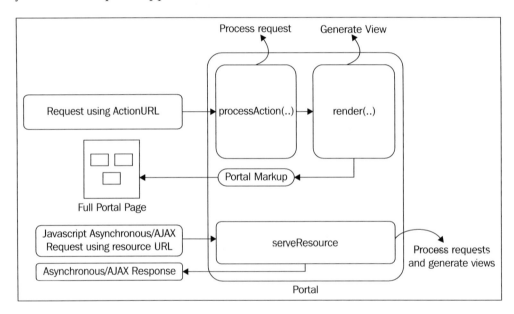

Hence, we can conclude that the following approaches are available for implementing a portlet user interface:

- For a traditional, JSR-168 based implementation, `ActionURL` and `RenderURL` are still options, although very limited ones, for asynchronous call implementations

- For an AJAX implementation and asynchronous request-response, the `ResourceURL` option offered by JSR-286, is the best.

JBoss 2.7.0 offers full support for the JSR-286 Portlet 2.0 specification, allowing us to implement robust AJAX-based applications without any workarounds.

With this background, let's dive right into developing a portlet for our "MyCompany" portal page using AJAX support. In subsequent sections, we will discuss the configuration and other in-built AJAX support provided by the JBoss portal server.

Developing an AJAX portlet

Let us enhance our sample application, the "MyCompany" portal, and implement AJAX functionality in one of the portlets, using asynchronous server calls and dynamic HTML.

We will build a simple asset allocation calculator which asks for the user's age and returns an asset allocation mix of stocks and bonds based on a simple age-based logic on the server side. The user interface will submit the request asynchronously to a portlet on the server, which will then process it and return a markup that will only refresh a segment of the page.

We will also use some special user interface DHTML effects to demonstrate the effective combination of asynchronous calls with a rich user interface.

The front-end

We will create a new portlet called "AJAXPortlet" in the "MyPortal" project, and position it in the center column below our current preferences portlet that we created in the last chapter.

The myportal-object.xml shows the following entry:

```
<deployments>
...
<deployment>
    <if-exists>overwrite</if-exists>
    <parent-ref>mycompany</parent-ref>
      <page>
            <page-name>default</page-name>
            <window>
                <window-name>MyCompany AJAX Portlet</window-name>
                <instance-ref>AJAXPortletInstance</instance-ref>
                <region>center</region>
                <height>2</height>
            </window>
        ...
      </page>
    </deployment>
</deployment>
```

Let's add our form to the JSP:

```
<!--AJAX submission via form
Actual post takes place in Javascript function -->
<form method='post'
      id="assetform"
      name="assetcalc"
      action=""
      onsubmit="ajaxSubmit('<%= renderResponse.
                  createResourceURL() %>','testdiv',
                  Form.serialize(this),true); return false;">
      <p>Your Age: <input type="text" name="age"/> <br><br>
      <input id="page" type="hidden" name="page" value="asset"/>
      <input id="submit" type="submit" name="Submit"/>
</form>
```

As we can see, the form has an `onSubmit` option to delegate submission to a JavaScript function. We are also using `ResourceURL`, generated from `renderResponse.createResourceURL()`, to submit our form. This allows us to talk directly to the portlet instead of to the portal. `testdiv` demarcates the location of the result.

 Although we are using the direct API here for illustrative purposes, we can use the Portlet 2.0 tag library provided by JBoss portal in our JSP, in which case the following `taglib` declaration needs to be added:
`<%@ taglib uri="http://java.sun.com/portlet_2_0" prefix="portlet" %>`

The `ResourceURL` looks like this:

```
/portal/portal/mycompany/default/MyCompany+AJAX+Portlet?action=b&cach
eability=PAGE
```

The `cacheability=PAGE` parameter indicates that we want the URL to contain the state of the complete page, including values such as `PortletURLs`, and so on.

Now, let's add some JavaScript code to process the form. It is useful to note that for an AJAX implementation, we rely on JavaScript functions to carry out our submissions and then track responses from the server asynchronously. Although we can write the JavaScript code ourselves, using existing popular libraries gives us a lot more efficiency and a broader feature set. We will use `scriptaculous.js` for the effects and `prototype.js` for asynchronous calls. These are available as standard in the headers of JBoss portal. Hence, we can use them without worrying about adding the library files along with the code. Our AJAX code includes asynchronous calls, and the special effects appear as follows:

```
<script type="text/javascript">
  // AJAX call using Prototype.js   and Scriptaculous for effects
  function ajaxSubmit(url,target,params,effects)
    {
        new Ajax.Updater(target, url, {method: 'GET', asynchronous:true,
                                          parameters:params});

        if(effects){
          new Effect.BlindDown(document.getElementById(target));
          new Effect.Highlight(document.getElementById(target),
          {startcolor: '#0066CC', endcolor: '#ffffff', restorecolor:
          '#FFCC99'});
        }
    }
</script>
```

Here, the `Ajax.Updater` function takes the `ResourceURL`, which is the target div for the results, and the parameters entered in the form, to make an asynchronous call to the server. If the effect is enabled, which it is in our example, when the server responds back with a markup, the JavaScript code will slide down, create space, and display the output, while highlighting the information in three colors for emphasis.

We are all set on the client side. Now let's go back and create our portlet.

The server-side portlet

Our JSP invokes an instance of `AJAXPortlet` which appears as follows:

```
public class AJAXPortlet extends GenericPortlet
{
    // async requests and responses are processed here
    public void serveResource(ResourceRequest req, ResourceResponse
    resp) throws PortletException, IOException
    {
        resp.setContentType("text/html");
        PrintWriter writer = resp.getWriter();
        String age = req.getParameter("age");
        if (age == null || age.equals("")){
          writer.print("<P> Sorry, Please enter valid age between
                        10 and 100! ");
        }
        else {
            String bond = age;
            int stock = 100 - Integer.parseInt(age);
            writer.print("<P>  The recommended asset allocation for
                        your age is: ");
            writer.print("<p> <b>Stocks: </b>" + stock + "%  <b> Bonds:
                        </b>" + bond + "%");
        }
```

```
        writer.close();
    }

    // parent page delivery
    public void render(RenderRequest renderRequest, RenderResponse
    renderResponse) throws PortletException, IOException
    {
        PortletContext context = getPortletContext();
        PortletRequestDispatcher rd = context.getRequestDispatcher
                                ("/WEB-INF/jsp/ajax_calc.jsp");
        rd.include(renderRequest, renderResponse);
    }
}
```

Let's look at this a bit more closely. The first method, `serveResource`, gets invoked when the JSP JavaScript performs a submission. We make a quick calculation, open a `PrintWriter` and write our output markup to it. The output of the `PrintWriter` goes directly back to the JavaScript call which then parses the information and displays it in the requested format. We also perform a quick validation of the input data to demonstrate how efficient it is to validate data by using AJAX.

Hence, using this single method, we have achieved asynchronous communication between a window on a client browser and a portlet.

The `render` method follows the traditional approach of serving the portlet window when the page first loads. All we do here is to point it to the JSP page that houses our AJAX calls.

Deployment

Once we build and deploy the portlet, and the home page is loaded, it looks like this:

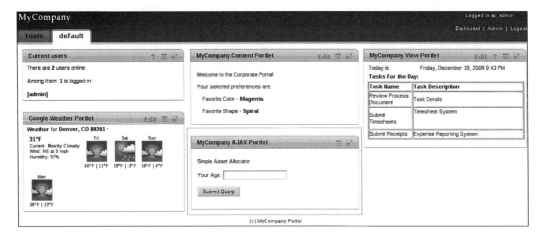

Let's enter some age as data in the field, and then submit the form.

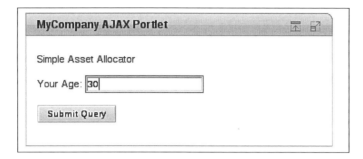

Once we enter the data and click on **Submit Query**, we should see the result showing up in the same page in a newly opened area below the portlet, and with some visual effects.

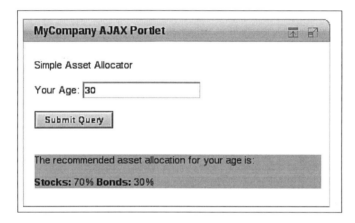

We can also see validation in action by entering either nothing or a number greater than 100. The server reinterprets the data and responds back with an error message, as shown below:

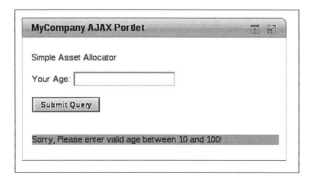

We just saw how simple and efficient it is to create AJAX-enabled portlets. Although, this was a simple example, fundamentally, as far as asynchronous call processing is concerned, most scenarios are likely to be very similar. However, the dynamic nature and rich content of the portlet user interface can be dramatically enhanced by adopting the latest DHTML/AJAX libraries.

Up until now, we have been talking about custom development. Let us now look at how JBoss portal leverages AJAX.

AJAX support for markup

JBoss portal supports markup through tags on layouts and renderers of the pages. Special tags are added to layout JSPs that facilitate the placement of AJAX features on a page. Similarly, renderers are used to interpret the tags and to render AJAX-driven content. The obvious advantage is the in-built support for the auto-creation and control of AJAX components on portal pages.

Layout markup

As discussed earlier, layouts provide a structure for the creation and serving of portal pages. Layouts aggregate all of the content generated by the portlet, based on region and order, merge them with some additional content provided by the portal, and serve a response back to the user. By providing support for AJAX in the layout, **helps** facilitate the easy development and implementation of dynamic functionality in pages, with minimal effort.

Layout markup is implemented using JSP tags. The JBoss JSP tag library, `portlet-layout.tld`, offers tags that facilitate the implementation of AJAX features in layouts. A JSP layout can be changed to an AJAX-supported page simply by adding references to the tags. Hence, using tags also helps with the easy implementation of features.

The following is the layout page from the default portal generic layout ${JBOSS_ PORTAL_HOME}\server\default\deploy\jboss-portal.sar\portal-core.war\ layouts\generic\index.jsp, and shows AJAX support implemented as tags:

```
<%@ page import="org.jboss.portal.server.PortalConstants" %>
<%@ taglib uri="/WEB-INF/theme/portal-layout.tld" prefix="p" %>
<!DOCTYPE html PUBLIC "-//W3C//DTD XHTML 1.0 Transitional//EN"
"http://www.w3.org/TR/xhtml1/DTD/xhtml1-transitional.dtd">
<html xmlns="http://www.w3.org/1999/xhtml">
<head>
    <title><%= PortalConstants.VERSION.toString() %></title>
    <meta http-equiv="Content-Type" content="text/html;"/>
    <!-- to correct the unsightly Flash of Unstyled Content. -->
```

```
    <script type="text/javascript"></script>
    <!-- inject the theme, default to the Renaissance theme if
            nothing is selected for the portal or the page -->
    <p:theme themeName="renaissance"/>
    <!-- insert header content that was possibly set by portlets
                                            on the page -->
    <p:headerContent/>
    <%@include file="/layouts/common/modal_head.jsp"%>
</head>

<body id="body">
<p:region regionName='AJAXScripts' regionID='AJAXScripts'/>
<%@include file="/layouts/common/modal_body.jsp"%>
<div id="portal-container">
    <div id="sizer">
        <div id="expander">
            <div id="logoName"></div>
            <table border="0" cellpadding="0" cellspacing="0"
                                    id="header-container">
                <tr>
                    <td align="center" valign="top" id="header">
                        <!-- Utility controls -->
                        <p:region regionName='dashboardnav' regionID=
                                            'dashboardnav'/>
                        <!-- navigation tabs and such -->
                        <p:region regionName=
                                    'navigation' regionID='navigation'/>
                        <div id="spacer"></div>
                    </td>
                </tr>
            </table>
            <div id="content-container">
                <!-- insert the content of the 'left' region of the page,
                        and assign the css selector id 'regionA' -->
                <p:region regionName='left' regionID='regionA'/>
                <!-- insert the content of the 'center' region of the
                        page, and assign the css selector id 'regionB' -->
                <p:region regionName='center' regionID='regionB'/>
                <hr class="cleaner"/>
            </div>
        </div>
    </div>
</div>

<div id="footer-container" class="portal-copyright">Powered by
```

```
<a class="portal-copyright" href="http://www.jboss.com/products/
jbossportal">JBoss Portal</a><br/>
</div>

<p:region regionName='AJAXFooter' regionID='AJAXFooter'/>

</body>
</html>
```

Renderer markup

The portal combines the renderers and layouts to generate the final content.
Enabling support for AJAX in the renderer just requires adding the statement
`<ajax-enabled>true</ajax-enabled>` to the renderer descriptor.

The following example, at `{JBOSS_PORTAL_HOME}\server\default\deploy\jboss-
portal.sar\portal-core.war\WEB-INF\layout\portal-renderSet.xml`, shows
the renderer configuration of the `emptyRenderer` RenderSet for AJAX support:

```
<renderSet name="emptyRenderer">
  <set content-type="text/html">
   <ajax-enabled>true</ajax-enabled>
   <region-renderer>
     org.jboss.portal.theme.impl.render.empty.EmptyRegionRenderer
   </region-renderer>
   <window-renderer>
     org.jboss.portal.theme.impl.render.empty.EmptyWindowRenderer
   </window-renderer>
   <portlet-renderer>
     org.jboss.portal.theme.impl.render.empty.EmptyPortletRenderer
   </portlet-renderer>
   <decoration-renderer>
     org.jboss.portal.theme.impl.render.empty.EmptyDecorationRenderer
   </decoration-renderer>
  </set>
</renderSet>
```

AJAX support for content

Whereas the layout and renderer contribute to AJAX behavior at the markup level,
JBoss portal's support for object-level configuration can be leveraged to provide
AJAX support at the page level. The object property inherits a configured behavior
from its parent. Currently, two features are offered for AJAX-driven content:

1. **Drag and drop**: Facilitates easy movement of portlets to various locations on screen using the mouse.

2. **Screen Refresh**: Allows sub-components of pages or individual portlets to refresh themselves without refreshing the entire page.

Drag-and-Drop

As the name suggests, this feature is triggered by a user action, and allows a portlet to detach itself from a specific location on the page and move to a different location on the page. This allows for the customization of the user interface to a form that is most convenient to the user. The dynamic view behavior comes from a combination of DHTML and asynchronous server-side communication.

Due to the nature of the behavior, drag-and-drop capability is available and effective only in dashboard pages where there are multiple portlets and the page layout can be personalized. The feature is allowed by default on the dashboard, but can be turned off by setting the value in the configuration file to `false`.

The following is a snippet of the default object configuration file (`jboss-portal. sar/conf/data/default-object.xml`), which illustrates the enabling of the feature. Please note that this can also be configured using the administration console user interface of the JBoss server.

```
<deployment>
    <if-exists>keep</if-exists>
    <context>
        <context-name>dashboard</context-name>
        <properties>
            ...
            <!-- Set the dnd property -->
            <property>
                <name>theme.dyna.dnd_enabled</name>
                <value>true</value>
            </property>
            ...
        </properties>
    </context>
</deployment>
```

`<name>theme.dyna.dnd_enabled</name>` value enables or disables the drag-and-drop behavior.

Partial content refresh

One of the most expensive processes in a portal is the **refresh** of portlets when the page is generated. For every user action on a page, the portal calls all of the portlet methods in a serial, but non-specific order, which involves a significant amount of time and server-side processing. Partial content refresh support mitigates these issues to a large extent with an effective use of client-server asynchronous communication. When the state of a single portlet changes, a partial content refresh facilitates the update and refresh of only that portlet, instead of for all of the portlets on the page. This prevents the regeneration of the whole page and the initialization of all of the portlets on the page.

The following image illustrates the partial content refresh flow:

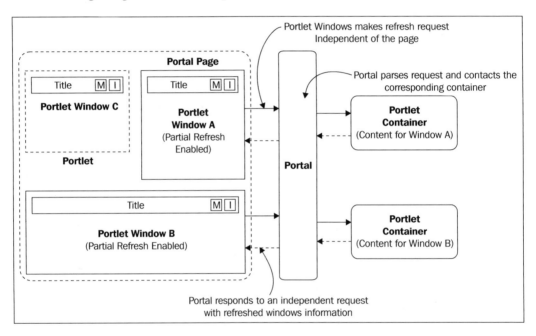

The partial refresh capability is compatible with the JSR-168 portlet API, which allows for programmatic update of portlet states during runtime.

Partial refreshes can be enabled through portal object configuration or through configuration at the default server level.

Portal object configuration

To implement partial page refreshes successfully, the properties of the portal objects need to be updated to include the property, `theme.dyna.partial_refresh_enabled`, which takes the values `true` or `false`. The deployment descriptor appears as follows:

```
<deployment>
    <if-exists>keep</if-exists>
    <context>
        <context-name>dashboard</context-name>
        <properties>
            ...
            <!-- Set the dnd property -->
            <property>
                <name>theme.dyna. partial_refresh_enabled</name>
                <value>true</value>
            </property>
            ...
        </properties>
    </context>
</deployment>
```

For changing the behavior during runtime, the property editor of the management portal can be used to set the values at the default server level. Once set, all of the pages in the portal automatically inherit the property. The default portal configuration is shown in the following screenshot:

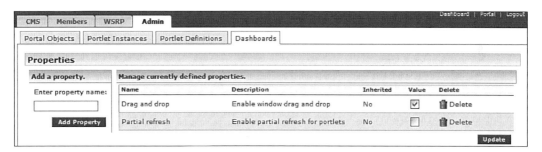

Portlet configuration

Although the default portal configuration enables partial refreshing for all portlets, it is also important to understand when a portlet would actually use a partial refresh. Having this knowledge helps us to control the behavior at the portlet level.

The server, by default, enables partial refresh for action and render links. However, there are the following exceptions for which the whole page is refreshed:

- Forms with GET requests. Using a GET request is discouraged by the portal specification. Hence, this should not be of significant concern.
- Form uploads.
- A window in a MAXIMIZED state. Partial page refreshes will not function when the window is entering or exiting a MAXIMIZED windows state.

There are, however, a few scenarios where we don't want to use a partial refresh at all. In such cases, partial refreshes can be disabled by using the following configuration in the portlet descriptor file, `jboss-portlet.xml`.

```
<portlet>
    <portlet-name>TestPortletBlockPartialRef</portlet-name>
    <ajax>
        <partial-refresh>false</partial-refresh>
    </ajax>
</portlet>
```

Setting the `<partial-refresh>` value to `false` prevents partial refreshes of portlets when they are invoked.

Constraints in implementing partial refresh

Although partial refresh is a powerful option, it has certain constraints on both the client and server sides.

Inconsistent session attributes

When a page is partially refreshed, the state of the page and its relationship to the portlets on the page become inconsistent. The direct impact of this is the session variables. If a partially-refreshed variable updates a session variable, a different portlet using this same variable will continue to use old data and might not be able to update to the latest session data.

In such cases, selective enabling of partial refreshes for portlets should address the problem.

Non-AJAX interaction

The AJAX implementation for partial refreshes is triggered by DOM events generated by the user in the browser. However, the user doesn't trigger these events. The portal JavaScript has no way of knowing the request, and hence might refresh the whole page.

A good example of this is the direct programmatic submission of forms, instead of relying on browser events for submission.

For issues like these, care should be taken when coding the portlets, and using constructs that do not generate DOM events should be avoided.

Considerations for AJAX implementations

Although AJAX is an exciting technology and provides significant advantages in terms of performance, usability, and implementation, there are certain scenarios where using AJAX is not a good fit. This is especially true when a lot of custom development is involved in using AJAX libraries.

Some of these are discussed in the following sections.

Global variables

One of the important aspects of portal-specific development is the obvious collision of variables declared at the global page level. Due to the nature of portals, a page typically consists of multiple portlets with their own local variables. Creating global variables almost invariably exposes the application to conflicts with local variables.

One solution might be to assign name spaces along with the variable declaration.

State management

With constant partial page refreshes happening, and content being refreshed through AJAX implementation, it is very difficult to keep the state of the page consistent. Page refreshes and content refreshes can occur at any given time, triggered by any portlet on a page. Hence, building a portlet with dependencies on a page can cause serious problems. Similar issues can crop up if a user uses the **Back** button on the browser.

All calls need to be atomic and should use techniques such as cookies to store states.

Visual cues

Users of web applications prefer to continuously receive the status on their actions, without which they tend to get impatient or nervous. Most AJAX functions and calls execute in the background with no obvious sign in the browser that the user needs to wait and that the browser is busy. Portals with multiple components on pages sometimes operate independently, further exacerbating the issue.

Hence, AJAX implementation should always use techniques that provide continuous visual cues to the user.

Summary

AJAX is a powerful tool. Used appropriately, it can provide tremendous value in terms of features, usability, performance, and implementation. The implementation is relatively native and simple with no need for special skills or plug-ins, other than the ones that web developers normally have. With the adoption of the Portlet 2.0 specification, AJAX development has become significantly easier and more reliable. Our example in this chapter showed how easy it is to develop and deploy AJAX-based portlets.

JBoss portal supplements custom development of portlets enriched with AJAX, with its own set of pre-packaged baked-in support for features such as AJAX-enabled layouts, drag-and-drops, partial refreshes, and so on. Portlets can be configured individually to provide or block AJAX features. Although it is powerful, it also comes with certain limitations. Developers can build a more robust portal solution using AJAX if they bear in mind these limitations.

In the next chapter, we will discuss how portlets can leverage persistent data stores and databases to build enterprise portal applications.

7
Databases and Portal

Databases today are an inseparable part of enterprise applications. Portals use databases both, internally to support portal server requirements, and also as a part of custom portlets written using a persistence mechanism. JBoss portal uses **Hibernate**, a very popular **Object Relationship Management (ORM)** tool, as its persistence provider. With its support for all major databases and powerful functionality that cleanly separates application code from database-specific implementations, Hibernate offers a strong model suitable for adoption for portal functionality.

In the next few sections, we will talk about how Hibernate is used internally by JBoss applications and how applications can integrate database support in portlet applications using Hibernate.

Database use in portal

Databases satisfy the primary need for persistence in most applications. They serve as a permanent store of information that can be accessed, referenced, edited, or deleted as and when required, beyond the scope of any user or the limitations of an application session. Portals are no exceptions. They, too, have the same need for persistent data storage and retrieval that databases provide.

JBoss portal server uses databases in a couple of ways:

- Internally, as a persistence store for configuration, sessions, state variables, user profiles, preferences, canned portlets, and so on
- As a part of portlet configuration created by custom code written specifically as a part of a portal application

In the coming sections, we will talk about how both of these are implemented.

Custom-developed portal applications, and portlets too, use databases for a large number of functions where data needs to be saved for use in the future. The `PortletSession` and the `PortletPreferences` are limited by capacity and function. Any data that is of substantial volume has to be persisted not only between sessions, but also for possible use outside of the portal environment, and has to be used in a relational database.

While discussing the portal server's database interactions, we will look at the how JBoss portal uses a tool called Hibernate (internally) to manage its persistent information and how portlet developers can effectively use Hibernate to build custom solutions.

Hibernate comes as a part of the libraries provided by JBoss portal, and the portal server already has its mappings and configuration defined for its internal use. Custom applications can use the libraries and just provide mappings and configuration as a part of their application. Before we dive into the details of how Hibernate and databases are used in JBoss portal, let us talk a bit about Hibernate.

Traditionally, database access in a portlet is coded using custom JDBC coding. However, as needs and complexity have increased, data mapping and ORM tools have taken over the function of database access, leaving portlet and application developers to focus on business functions. In this chapter, we will discuss custom portlet development using databases, primarily using the Hibernate ORM tool.

Hibernate

Hibernate is one of the leading open source object relationship mapping solutions available in the industry today. Object relationship mapping tools act as a bridge between an object-oriented model of a Java/JEE application and relational databases. Hibernate offers a set of tools and an API that allow application domain objects to map to database tables (including relationships and constraints), to manage database session access and application transactionality.

JBoss portal server has adopted Hibernate as the preferred tool for ORM functionality and database access for portal implementations.

Hibernate's primary strength lies in its strong database access functions using simple POJOs as persistent classes that map to database tables by using configurable XML files or annotations. The persistent POJO classes can be used across the domain tier. Hibernate can be configured to manage connections to the database, or can access JNDI for container-managed connections. Similarly, it can work both with local transactions and container-managed transactions, including distributed transactions.

Typical steps in using Hibernate in applications are as follows:

1. Create POJO persistent classes with attributes
2. Set Hibernate properties, including database configuration
3. Create a Hibernate mapping file to map persistent class attributes to database table values
4. Write DAO code that leverages persistent classes

In the next few sections, we will examine how the portal server leverages Hibernate. We will later explore the creation of custom portal applications using Hibernate.

JBoss portal server using Hibernate

Earlier, we discussed how JBoss portal server uses databases internally for various functions. Now let's see how it uses Hibernate to work with the database, to store configuration information, session or state information, persist preferences, and other data.

Hibernate configuration for portal features

For practically all of the database interactions, JBoss portal uses Hibernate internally for persistence and ORM functionality. The portal server's Hibernate configuration are stored in the directory `$JBOSS_PORTAL_HOME/server/default/deploy/jboss-portal.sar/conf/hibernate`.

Separate Hibernate configurations and mapping files can be found for portal instance, portal, portlet, user, and workflow functions of the portal.

Moreover, these configurations rely on Hibernate `SessionFactory` components that are created in `SessionFactoryBinder`, and Mbeans defined in `jboss-portal.sar/META-INF/jboss-service.xml`.

JBoss portal uses the HSQL database internally, but is recommended only for development servers. For production and other managed environments, it strongly recommended that other fully-fledged databases are used. Currently, the portal platform has been tested on MySQL 4 and 5, Microsoft SQL Server, PostgreSQL 8, and Oracle Database 9/10. Due to Hibernate's support for multiple databases, the transition between databases is seamless, and the server re-generates all of the database relationships when databases are switched. Only the configuration files and dialects need to be updated to match the appropriate database software.

In clustered configurations, the portal uses Hibernate's clustering configurations to replicate the caches used by Hibernate across multiple servers in the cluster to maintain consistency and state.

```
<!--
| Uncomment in clustered mode : use transactional replicated cache
-->
<property name="cache.provider_class">
    org.jboss.portal.core.hibernate.JMXTreeCacheProvider
</property>
<property name="cache.object_name">
    portal:service=TreeCacheProvider,type=hibernate
</property>
<!--
| Comment in clustered mode
<property name="cache.provider_configuration_file_resource_path">
    conf/hibernate/instance/ehcache.xml
</property>
<property name="cache.provider_class">
    org.hibernate.cache.EhCacheProvider
</property>
-->
```

Content management system database storage

There are multiple ways of storing information in content management systems. However, many times, for efficiency and performance related reasons, content management systems use databases to persist information related to displayable content, configuration, and meta tags in the database. JBoss portal server leverages Hibernate to access these databases.

In addition, although there are alternative options for storing contents in the file system, using Hibernate makes it easier for the CMS application to access the database effectively and efficiently.

To edit the default configuration, the file `$JBOSS_PORTAL_HOME/server/default/deploy/jboss-portal.sar/portal-cms.sar/META-INF/jboss-service.xml` is used.

Building portlets using Hibernate

Hibernate has been extensively used in J2EE applications for quite some time now, and many have realized its benefits and value. Creating portlets using Hibernate follows the same approach. A lot of portlets require database access for their functionality. Having a versatile and robust tool like Hibernate, and using it in the development of a portlet, can provide tremendous benefit both in terms of application efficiency, as well as quality. Portlet applications can now be built much more quickly and with ease. The pattern prescribed by Hibernate usage, complemented by the high quality SQL generated by Hibernate, results in strong, sustainable applications.

In the next few sections, we will be going into the details of creating portlets using Hibernate and then deploying them on the server.

A persistent portlet

Now that we have seen how JBoss portal uses Hibernate internally, let us see how we can use Hibernate for creating custom portlet applications.

For our example, we will create a simple vacation approval system. This is a typical application on the corporate Intranet, and its basic functionality is to view and approve vacation time. The manager retrieves the vacation request of an associate in the company, who reports to him by using his employee ID, reviews the vacation dates, and then proceeds to approve or deny the request.

We will use Hibernate for all of our interactions with the database, following the steps outlined earlier for creating the application.

Configuring and using Hibernate

Using Hibernate in portlet development follows all of the steps of development of a typical J2EE application, plus some additional steps to integrate with the portal. The latter is the same for any of the portlet deployments discussed in the earlier chapters.

The steps for development are as follows:

1. Create a persistent class called `User`, which will retain information for CRUD (create, read, update, delete) operations with the database.

2. Configure the database and populate it with data. We will use a Hypersonic SQL database for our simple needs. Given that the database is used by the JBoss server, we will not have to install any new binaries to execute our code.

3. Create a Hibernate mapping file named `Employee.hbm.xml`, mapping the persistent class to the database tables. In our simple case, we will be dealing with a single database table to read from and write information to.

4. Configure Hibernate in the `hibernate.cfg.xml` file, specifying the database connections, dialects, and mapping files.

5. Write the DAO class file, which works with the Hibernate session to read and save persistent classes. The portlet class will delegate all of the database processing to the DAO class.

6. Create `DbPortlet` and configure it through the portlet configurations.

7. Package the classes and configuration file, including portlet configurations, as a WAR file.

8. Deploy the WAR file on the portal server and test.

Let us look at each step in detail.

Creating the persistent class

Our persistent class is a simple POJO with properties that describe the employee and vacation details. The class will be mapped to the database tables and is used by the DAO, supported by Hibernate, to persist or retrieve employee information from the database in the form of a Java class, instead of a `ResultSet`. Given that the class is a plain POJO with no dependencies, it can be safely used across tiers.

The following is the complete listing of the class:

```
package org.mycompany.portlet.db.domain;

public class Employee {
    private String employeeId;
    private String firstName;
    private String lastName;
    private String vacationDuration;
    private int approval;

    public Employee() {
        super();
    }

    public Employee(String employeeId, String firstName, String
                lastName, String vacationDuration, int approval) {
        super();
        this.employeeId = employeeId;
        this.firstName = firstName;
        this.lastName = lastName;
        this.vacationDuration = vacationDuration;
        this.approval = approval;
    }
}
```

```
    public String getEmployeeId() {
       return employeeId;
    }
    public void setEmployeeId(String employeeId) {
       this.employeeId = employeeId;
    }
    public String getFirstName() {
       return firstName;
    }
    public void setFirstName(String firstName) {
       this.firstName = firstName;
    }
    public String getLastName() {
       return lastName;
    }
    public void setLastName(String lastName) {
       this.lastName = lastName;
    }
    public String getVacationDuration() {
       return vacationDuration;
    }
    public void setVacationDuration(String vacationDuration) {
       this.vacationDuration = vacationDuration;
    }
    public int getApproval() {
       return approval;
    }
    public void setApproval(int approval) {
       this.approval = approval;
    }
}
```

Setting up database

For our example, we are going to use a **Hypersonic SQL database (HSQLDB)**. HSQLDB is a very simple database providing options for storing data both in memory and in the file system. The in-memory data is obviously transient in nature, but the file system database saves the data on the hard disk. We will use the file system to save our tables and the database records in them. As JBoss server uses HSQLDB internally, using it in our example will not require us to include binaries for different database software during build time or when deploying our application.

Please note that this is purely for illustrative purposes, used in our example for demonstrating the use of databases in portals. Even though in reality production systems use bigger, better, and full-featured RDBMS databases such as Oracle, SQLServer, MySQL, and so on, the process shown here can easily be adopted for these databases. The advantage of using an ORM tool such as Hibernate is that, with minimal configuration changes, databases can be switched from small to large.

It will be useful to put our HSQLDB in the context of enterprise databases when considering our example, as the differences aren't significant from code and portlet implementation perspective.

To use HSQLDB in our example, we need to create a database and populate it with some test data.

HSQLDB comes with a pretty nifty database manager, which we can use to create our table and insert a few rows.

After starting the database manager, let us enter the SQL to create a new table called **JBOSSPORTAL**.

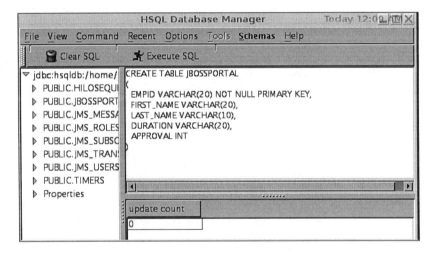

HSQLDB creates all of the data definitions and data, under the `data` directory, under the database root.

We have the employee ID as the primary key, along with the first name, last name, duration of the vacation requested, and a flag to denote whether the leave was approved.

Let's go ahead and add a couple of rows of data so that we have something to play with, when our portlet is ready.

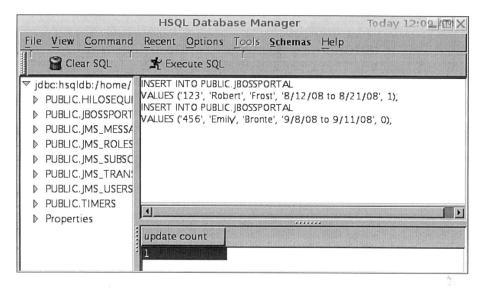

The following is a basic outline of the database structure:

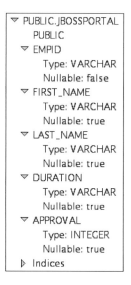

Creating the mappings

Hibernate uses a mapping file, defined as `*.hbm.xml`, which maps the persistent class attributes to database column names. This file is also used to define the association between tables. For our example, we will be using a single table with a single primary key. Hence, no mappings are used.

```xml
<?xml version="1.0" encoding="utf-8"?>
<!DOCTYPE hibernate-mapping PUBLIC "-//Hibernate/Hibernate Mapping DTD
3.0//EN"
"http://hibernate.sourceforge.net/hibernate-mapping-3.0.dtd">
<hibernate-mapping>
    <class name="org.mycompany.portlet.db.domain.Employee"
        table="JBOSSPORTAL">
        <id
            name="employeeId"
            column="EMPID">
        <generator class="assigned"/>
        </id>
        <property
            name="firstName"
            column="FIRST_NAME"/>
    <property
            name="lastName"
            column="LAST_NAME"/>
    <property
            name="vacationDuration"
            column="DURATION"/>
    <property
            name="approval"
            column="APPROVAL"/>
    </class>
</hibernate-mapping>
```

Configuring Hibernate

Hibernate configuration is stored in a file called `hibernate.cf.xml`, which is stored at the root of the Java source. Storing it in the `classes` directory will ensure that it is read. In this file, we declare the database connections, define the appropriate drivers to be used, the dialects to be chosen, and most importantly, the mapping files to be used. We can also use this file to define connection pools.

In our case, we are using an HSQLDB database with managed local connections. The database location is mentioned as `/projects/data/localDB`, but this can be changed to the one that best suits the environment.

As we can see, we are referencing the `employee.hbm.xml` file for mapping our classes to the database table.

```xml
<?xml version='1.0' encoding='UTF-8'?>
<!DOCTYPE hibernate-configuration PUBLIC
        "-//Hibernate/Hibernate Configuration DTD 3.0//EN"
        "http://hibernate.sourceforge.net/hibernate-configuration-
        3.0.dtd">

<hibernate-configuration>
  <session-factory>
      <property name="hibernate.connection.driver_class">
         org.hsqldb.jdbcDriver
      </property>
      <property name="connection.url">
         jdbc:hsqldb:/projects/data/localDB
      </property>
      <property name="hibernate.connection.username">sa</property>
      <property name="hibernate.connection.password"></property>
      <property name="show_sql">true</property>
      <property name="cache.use_second_level_cache">true</property>
      <property name="cache.use_query_cache">false</property>
     <!-- property name="hibernate.hbm2ddl.auto">update</property -->
      <property name="dialect">
         org.hibernate.dialect.HSQLDialect
      </property>
      <property name="cache.provider_class">
         org.hibernate.cache.EhCacheProvider
      </property>

      <!-- Mapping files -->
      <mapping resource="org/mycompany/portlet/db/employee.hbm.xml"/>
  </session-factory>
</hibernate-configuration>
```

Creating the Data Access Object class

Next, we define the **Data Access Object (DAO)** class that pulls the POJO classes and the mappings together, by defining methods that read from and write to the database. A DAO class abstracts the persistence details from the application and facilitates communication between the application and the database.

The `getEmployee (String id)` method gives us an `Employee` object when the employee ID is supplied. Similarly, the `setEmployee(String approval, String empId)` method retrieves the employee record associated with the employee ID, and updates the decision on the vacation request.

It is also important to note that we start Hibernate sessions to perform database operations. We also wrap database updates in Hibernate-managed transactions, to ensure atomic transactions.

```
package org.mycompany.portlet.db;

import org.mycompany.portlet.db.domain.Employee;
import org.hibernate.*;
import org.hibernate.cfg.*;
public class EmployeeDAO {
    public EmployeeDAO() {
        super();
    }
    public Employee getEmployee(String id) {
        SessionFactory factory = new Configuration().configure()
                           .buildSessionFactory();
        Session session = factory.openSession();
        try{
            Employee emp = (Employee) session.get( Employee.class,
                           id.trim());

            return emp;
        }
        finally {
            session.close();
        }
    }

    public long setEmployee(String approval, String empId) {
        SessionFactory factory = new Configuration().configure()
                           .buildSessionFactory();
        Session session = factory.openSession();
        try{
            // start transaction as this is an update
            Transaction trans = session.beginTransaction();
            // load transient copy of the class
            Employee emp = (Employee) session.load(Employee.class,
                           empId);
            emp.setApproval(Integer.valueOf(approval).intValue());
            session.update(emp);
            // update database
            trans.commit();

            return 0;
        }
          finally {
            session.close();
          }
    }
}
```

The Portlet class and configuration

We will also create a new portlet class titled `DbPortlet.java`, which will route requests to and from the portlet. As we can see from the following code snippet, based on the page information passed as a parameter by the portlet, the `processAction` calls the appropriate method on the DAO class:

```java
public class DbPortlet extends GenericPortlet {

    private PortletContext portletContext;

    // Add all logic related to submitted forms, responses and
    //   actions
    // Pretty much default method for all functions, except edit and
    //   help
    public void init(PortletConfig config) throws PortletException {
        super.init(config);
        portletContext = config.getPortletContext();
    }

    public void doView(RenderRequest request,RenderResponse response)
        throws PortletException,IOException {
        String contentPage = getContentJSP(request);

        response.setContentType(request.getResponseContentType());
        if (contentPage != null && contentPage.length() != 0) {
            try {
                PortletRequestDispatcher dispatcher = portletContext.
                                getRequestDispatcher(contentPage);
                dispatcher.include(request, response);
            } catch (IOException e) {
                throw new PortletException("ViewPortlet.doView
                    exception", e);
            }
        }

    }

    // Use this method to add logic to "Edit" function
    // For example, show the appropriate edit page
    // Note: Any actions when the edit page is submitted, go in the
    //   doView() method
    public void doEdit(RenderRequest request,RenderResponse response)
        throws PortletException {

    }

    // Use this method to add logic to "Help" function
    // For example, show the appropriate help page, based on context
    public void doHelp(RenderRequest request,RenderResponse response)
        throws PortletException {
```

```java
        }
    public void processAction (ActionRequest request, ActionResponse
    actionResponse)
    throws PortletException, java.io.IOException {
    // instantiate DAO class
    EmployeeDAO empDAO = new EmployeeDAO();
    String empId = (String) request.getParameter("empId");
    String page = (String) request.getParameter("page");
    if (page != null && page.equals("vacation")) {
        // fetch entire employee record
        Employee emp = empDAO.getEmployee(empId);
         // return response
        String response ="";
        if (emp != null) {
           response = emp.getEmployeeId() + "," + emp.getFirstName()
                    + "," + emp.getLastName() + "," + emp.
                    getVacationDuration()+ "," + emp.getApproval();
        }
        //actionResponse.setPortletMode(PortletMode.VIEW);
        actionResponse.setRenderParameters(request.getParameterMap());
        actionResponse.setRenderParameter("employee", response);
    } else {
        if (page != null && page.equals("approval")) {
          String approval = (String) request.getParameter
                            ("approval");
          if (approval.equals("Approve")) {
            empDAO.setEmployee("1", empId);
          } else if (approval.equals("Deny")) {
            empDAO.setEmployee("0", empId);
            }
        actionResponse.setRenderParameters(request.getParameterMap());
          }
        }
    }
    protected String getContentJSP(RenderRequest request)
            throws PortletException {
    String page = (String) request.getParameter("page");
    if(page != null && page.equals("vacation")) {
        return "/WEB-INF/jsp/id_vacation.jsp";
    } else if(page != null && page.equals("approval")) {
        return "/WEB-INF/jsp/approval.jsp";
      } else {
        return "/WEB-INF/jsp/enterid.jsp";
      }
    }
}
```

Just as we did for all of our portlets, we also need to configure our DbPortlet so that it gets deployed along with our portal application.

We create the appropriate entry in portlet.xml as follows:

```
<portlet>
        <portlet-name>DbPortlet</portlet-name>
        <portlet-class>org.mycompany.portlet.db.DbPortlet</portlet-
         class>
        <supports>
            <mime-type>text/html</mime-type>
            <portlet-mode>VIEW</portlet-mode>
        </supports>
        <portlet-info>
            <title>Db Portlet</title>
        </portlet-info>
    </portlet>
```

Then instantiate it in portlet-instance.xml, as follows:

```
<deployment>
        <instance>
            <instance-id>DbPortletInstance</instance-id>
            <portlet-ref>DbPortlet</portlet-ref>
        </instance>
</deployment>
```

We can then define its layout, theme, and RenderSet in the mycompany-object.xml file, as follows:

```
<deployment>
        <if-exists>overwrite</if-exists>
        <parent-ref>mycompany.default</parent-ref>
                <window>
            <window-name>DbPortletWindow</window-name>
            <instance-ref>DbPortletInstance</instance-ref>
            <region>center</region>
            <height>0</height>
        </window>
        <properties>
            <property>
            <name>layout.id</name>
            <value>mycompany_threecol</value>
            </property>
            <property>
            <name>theme.renderSetId</name>
            <value>emptyRenderer</value>
            </property>
        </properties>
    </deployment>
```

As we can see, the **DbPortlet** window is defined as the topmost window, in the center column.

Building and deployment

The build script will generate the deployable WAR file. The portlet class and the persistent class are packaged along with the configuration, and the WAR file is deployed on the server.

```
C:\WINXP\system32\cmd.exe                                              _ □ ×

C:\projects\MyCompanyPortal>ant
Buildfile: build.xml

clean:
    [delete] Deleting directory C:\projects\MyCompanyPortal\output
    [delete] Deleting directory C:\projects\MyCompanyPortal\src\resources\mycompa
ny-war\WEB-INF\lib
    [delete] Deleting directory C:\projects\MyCompanyPortal\src\resources\mycompa
ny-war\WEB-INF\classes

prepare:
    [mkdir] Created dir: C:\projects\MyCompanyPortal\output\classes
    [mkdir] Created dir: C:\projects\MyCompanyPortal\output\lib
    [mkdir] Created dir: C:\projects\MyCompanyPortal\output\lib\exploded

build:
    [javac] Compiling 5 source files to C:\projects\MyCompanyPortal\output\class
es
    [copy] Copying 1 file to C:\projects\MyCompanyPortal\output\classes
    [copy] Copying 1 file to C:\projects\MyCompanyPortal\output\classes\org\myc
ompany\portlet\db
    [mkdir] Created dir: C:\projects\MyCompanyPortal\src\resources\mycompany-war
\WEB-INF\lib
    [mkdir] Created dir: C:\projects\MyCompanyPortal\src\resources\mycompany-war
\WEB-INF\classes
    [copy] Copying 7 files to C:\projects\MyCompanyPortal\src\resources\mycompa
ny-war\WEB-INF\classes
    [copy] Copying 1 file to C:\projects\MyCompanyPortal\src\resources\mycompan
y-war\WEB-INF\lib
     [jar] Building jar: C:\projects\MyCompanyPortal\mycompany.war

BUILD SUCCESSFUL
Total time: 1 second
C:\projects\MyCompanyPortal>
```

We can now test the applications and see Hibernate work with the portlet to generate and retrieve database content.

Now that the portlet has been deployed along with the others in our example, "MyCompany" portal, let's test it out.

When the portal loads, we can see the **Db Portlet** in the center column, as described in the configurations, with an input field that is used to enter the **Employee Id**. Let us enter the employee ID we used as test data.

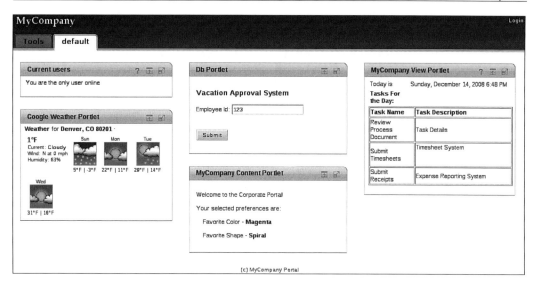

After the request has been submitted, the portlet uses the employee ID to retrieve the employee's record, which includes the details of the employee and the proposed vacation dates, from the database. As we can see, the portlet now has an option for the manager to either **Approve** or **Deny** the absence.

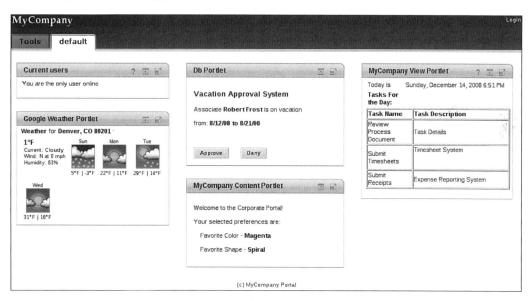

Let's approve the employee's vacation. Once the **Approve** button is clicked, the portlet submits the decision, along with the employee's ID. The DAO class retrieves existing database record for the employee by using the employee ID and then updates the decision in the employee's record. The portlet eventually provides the following confirmation screen:

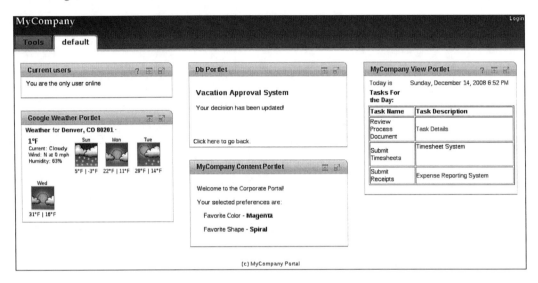

Summary

Today, databases are used everywhere. The importance of databases in today's application is significant. Like regular enterprise applications, portal applications tend to leverage databases to a significant extent. JBoss portal uses databases for internal use, and also supports custom portlet applications deployed on the server.

Hibernate is a popular and powerful ORM tool, which makes the interactions with database easier, efficient, and high-performing. As the responsibility of SQL generation, the writing of cumbersome SQL code, and so on are delegated to Hibernate, portlet developers can concentrate on writing strong domain logic.

Until now, we have been talking about the programmatic implementation of portal solutions. In the next chapter, we will discuss another important aspect of portals, that relates to how we can create and manage content using the content management system features of JBoss portal effectively and efficiently.

8
Managing Content in Portal

Portal applications deal with a large amount of content which requires efficient management, publishing, and delivery. Due to the personalized nature of a portal, along with applications, users expect a single source for information. Hence, it is natural to expect portals to contain content management system for timely and effective creation, approvals, and delivery.

JBoss portal server offers a powerful, secure, and feature-rich content management solution that enables us to create and manage content on our portal application. JBoss portal content management system is not an alternative to standalone and dedicated content management system that enterprise use for various other purposes. However, it provides sufficient features to effectively manage content in a portal application. In this chapter, we will review the features of the portal's content management system and then try them out with examples.

Content management systems

A **Content Management System (CMS)** is defined as an application that helps to create, edit, manage, and deliver web site content in a consistent and reliable manner. Imagine creating, editing, and publishing a typical corporate web site manually, with hundreds or thousands of pieces of content. A CMS is a system born out of the need for automating the management of the life cycle of content on large web sites. A CMS allows the shifting of responsibility of managing web site content from technical resources such as programmers and developers, to the actual owners and stakeholders of the content. A good CMS system separates content from layout and presentation to provide business users with an infrastructure that they can use to create, edit, approve, and publish content without worrying about how it will be laid out on an HTML page. It provides options to version content, send content through an approval workflow, and define automated publishing times without unnecessary technical intervention. This not only improves efficiency, but also ensures content freshness and prevents the loss of message in translation, both literally and figuratively, resulting in a process that gives control back to the business users who actually own the content.

CMS has a distinct place in the enterprise application portfolio today, and there are vendors who offer standalone CMS software with fully-fledged services and advanced features. Portal servers invariably include CMS features to provide comprehensive support for managing content. Even though the CMS features provided by portals are not as extensive as fully-fledged standalone CMS products, it is sufficient to fulfill the needs of a typical portal user.

JBoss portal offers support for content management through a portlet implementation that provides specialized capabilities such as content creation, editing, storage, delivery, and some limited workflow management. It also provides in-built support for localization.

To implement content and repository management, JBoss portal uses **Apache Jackrabbit**. Jackrabbit is an open source product focused on serving as a content repository for the Java platform. It provides a large number of features that are preferred from an effective content repository, such as access control, versioning, clustering, locking, and so on. Jackrabbit, provides a series of API and configuration files that can be customized to fit specific needs. JBoss portal uses these options to work with Jackrabbit.

Let us delve a bit deeper into the features offered by JBoss portal by first looking at the CMS from a user's perspective, with an example, before looking at other configuration options on the server.

We can start managing content using JBoss portal CMS by following three basic steps:

1. Create content
2. Define a location for this content
3. Edit and adjust the content on a page, as needed

In the next few sections, we will review these steps in detail. Our goal is to add some new content to our "MyCompany" portal home page, and to display this content in its own CMS window. We should also be able to edit and manipulate the page contents when we need to.

Adding content to portal

The best way to understand the way that the portal CMS functions is to try it out with an example. In this example, we will add some new content to the portal on its own URL by importing an existing project tree. Alternatively, we can create all of the pages from scratch. However, it would be much more realistic to create a content tree with HTML, CSS, and image files generated using our favorite editor and then load an archive of these files to the portal.

For our example, we will take a simple content tree with a couple of HTML files, a style sheet, and an image. The content of our file `cms.zip` will appear as follows:

```
cms\
cms\images
cms\css
cms\images\logo4.png
cms\css\html.css
cms\testlink.html
cms\index.html
```

Once we log on to the portal as an administrator, the **Admin** link on the upper right takes us to a panel with four tabs on it. The first tab is **CMS,** and on clicking on it, we are taken to the following screenshot:

As we can see, there is currently only one directory, called **default**, listed. This is the default portal web site with the index page for the default tree serving as the base home page.

We will now select an action from the drop-down button at the top of the screen and try to import the project archive that we created earlier. Alternatively, as we discussed earlier, we could also create a directory manually and create each individual file within it, but for the sake of convenience, we will use a directory tree with content and images already created and packaged as a ZIP file.

Selecting the **Upload Archive** option brings us to the following screenshot:

We pick the archive cms.zip from the file system by using the **Browse...** button. It is important that the archive is created at the root directory level, and includes the root directory, with the subdirectory structure being retained. In other words, the content files should be packaged under a single root—**cms** in this case. The portal loads the directory and deploys it behind the scenes. If we now go back to the home page of CMS admin, we should see that the server has exploded the archive with the root directory **cms** now at the same level as the **default** directory, as shown in the following screenshot:

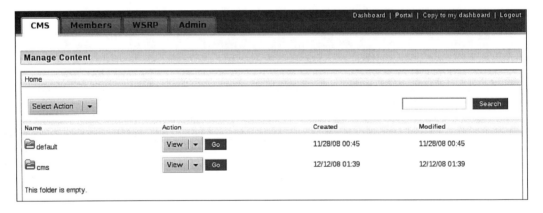

Clicking on the **cms** directory link gives us the listing of the subdirectories and files as they were originally packaged in the ZIP file, as shown in the following screenshot:

With this, we have now added content to the portal, and this content is ready for use on the portal page. We now need to define the location or window that this content will go into.

Adding content to portal pages

We are going to pick our ongoing example of "MyCompany", and the newly-added content in the center column of the layout.

We first need to create a window for the portal server to recognize the content. To add the content to our home page, we have to go back to the "MyCompany" layout section on the **Admin | Portal Objects** page. Once we are on the layout page, we need to select **cms** as the **Content Type**. This is a special content type defined by the JBoss portal that allows the rendering of managed content.

As soon as this option is selected, the server will present all of the content that has been added to the system. We should see the `cms` directory along with **default** one. Clicking on the **cms** link will expand its contents. Let's go ahead and specify that we want to add the `index.html` page of the ZIP archive that we have uploaded and added to the "MyCompany" home page. Once the file has been selected, the screen appears as shown below:

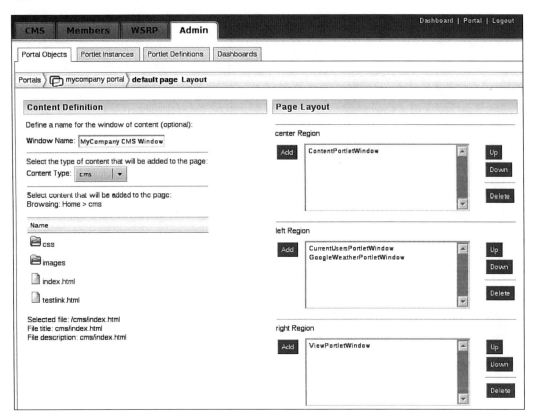

We will call our window **MyCompany CMS Window**, just to be explicit for demonstration purposes. The window name is optional. Given that we want the content in the central layout, we need to click the **Add** button in the **center Region** and re-order **MyCompany CMS Window** to make it the topmost entry.

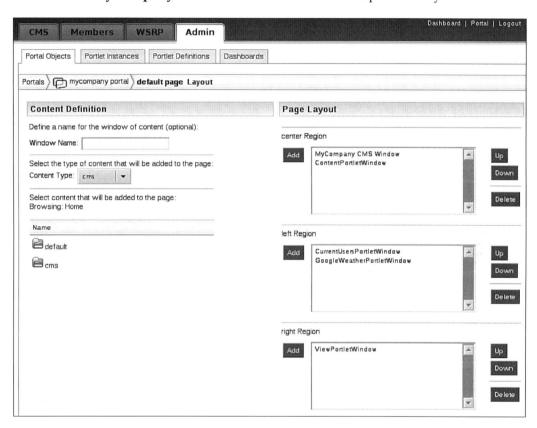

That's it! We are all set now. Let's go to our **MyCompany** home page and look at our changes:

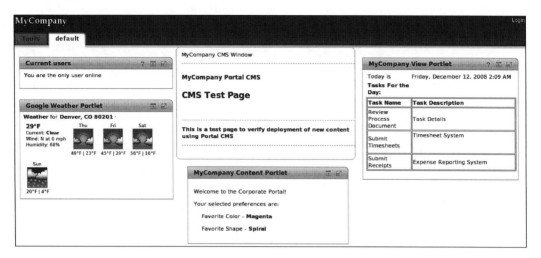

We can now see the contents of cms\index.html highlighted in the center column of the **MyCompany** home page. Moreover, it is worthwhile noting that, unlike other portlet windows, the CMS window doesn't have decorations or borders. This is purely to facilitate easy assimilation of plain content on portal pages.

Now that we have the page working, let's explore the editing capabilities of the portal server. Let's add a new hyperlink to the page, to connect to another page we uploaded in the archive.

Editing content

To edit the page, we go back to the **CMS** tab in the admin console and click on the **cms** directory that we uploaded earlier. It should look like the following screenshot:

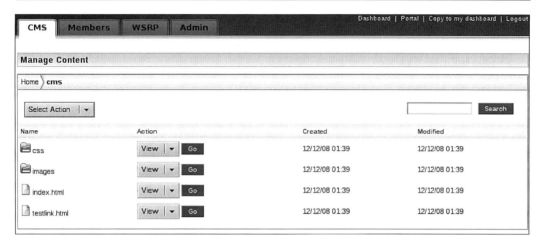

Let's click on the `index.html` file that we want to edit:

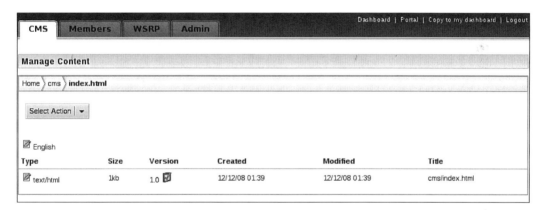

We can see that the file is in its first version. The in-built version control lists all of the versions of the index page for the **cms** folder. To edit the file, we can use any version. However, in our case, we will use the first version available.

The portal now displays an editor screen with options to edit the meta information of the page, and the contents of the page. A **WYSIWYG** HTML editor loads the page in an editable form, ready for any changes. Please note that some of the controls we see in the WYSIWYG editor vary in behavior with different browsers, and in some cases, you may have to tweak the HTML manually.

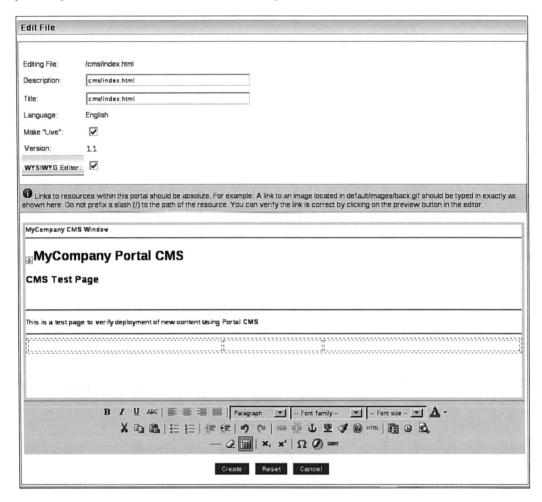

The screen provides all of the options needed to create an HTML page, without writing a single line of HTML.

Let's go ahead and edit the page by adding a reference link to the testlink.html page we uploaded as part of the cms.zip file.

Once we highlight the text that we want to make a link and click on the **Create** option, a small window pops up where we can define all of the configuration options for the link. In our case here, we have added an explicit link to the file, **testlink.html**.

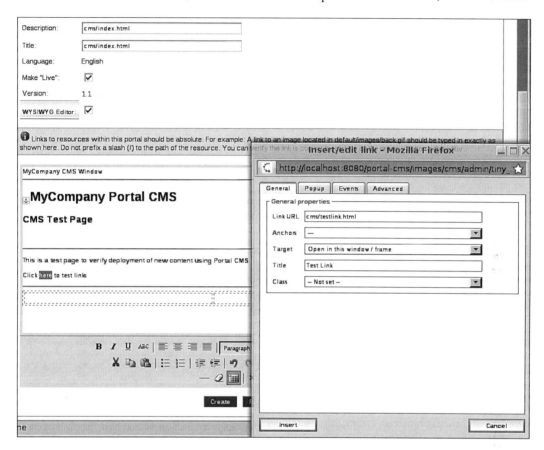

Once the link has been added, click on the **Create** button to create a newer version of the file for the version control records.

At this point, before we save the page, we also have an option not to make the content live immediately. By deselecting the **Make Live** option in the top section of the page, the server makes the edits, and versions it, but doesn't deploy the changes. Later, when we are ready, we can edit the page again to make it live. In our case, we will keep the checkbox selected to test the changes right away.

With our changes saved, the index.html file now has a newer version as indicated by the version being updated to **1.1**; the checkmark icon indicates that this is the live version of the file.

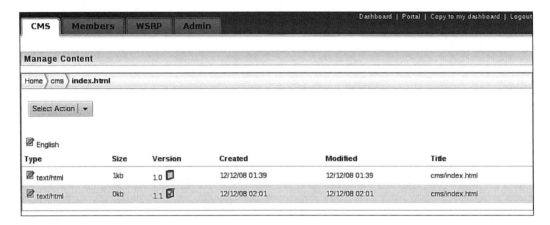

Now, let's go back and display the home page again. We can now see that the new line with the link has been added:

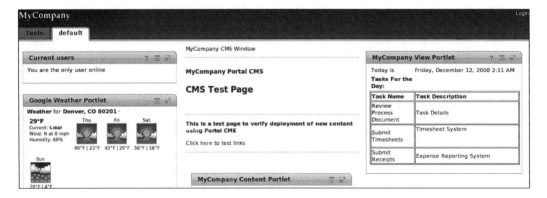

Clicking on the link takes us to the `testlink.html` page of the `cms` directory.

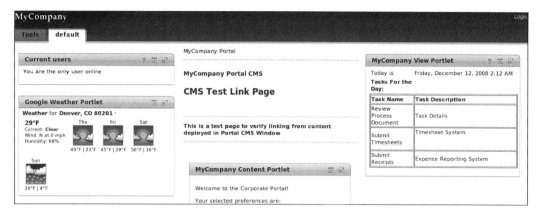

By using a simple example, we have now seen how easy it is to create, edit, and manage content on the JBoss portal. For scenarios that require the creation of new web pages and web content, using the in-built CMS is the best option. The JBoss Portal User Guide offers more details on all of the available configuration options that are available for better administering the CMS system.

However, being a portal, sometimes there may be scenarios where we want to manage content not on a page, but within a custom portlet. The CMS portlet, along with CMS Admin portlet, manages the content management services for the JBoss portal. Although we can use the user interface provided via the console, we can build much diverse functionality by leveraging the capabilities of the CMS portlet and the CMS admin portlet

The CMS portlet

We have already seen the features and administrative functionality provided by the CMS Admin portlet using the console. The CMS portlet facilitates navigation of portal content such as HTML, images, binary files, and so on, and is responsible for serving them. It uses a path mapper to map content to specific URLs prefixed with `/content`, and has the capability to serve content based on locale settings. A page for a preferred language is first retrieved from the file system, failing which, the portlet displays the default English version.

All non-binary content is displayed within the portal window, whereas binary content such as images, documents, and so on, are displayed completely outside of the portlet window.

A CMS portlet content delivery mechanism results in the following features:

- Content can be localized based on the preference of the user
- Binary content can be served outside of the portal on a simple URL such as `http://domain/content/logo.gif`
- Content is delivered through URLs that are distinct, small, and simple, making them user and search-engine friendly, for example, `http://domain/[portal]/content/index.html`
- Page configuration and layout is easy

Displaying CMS content is pretty straightforward. Just like the various content types we covered in earlier chapters, JBoss portal provides a special content type called **cms**, which effectively takes care of reading and serving the appropriate content for the portal.

The configuration, like other content types, is done in the deployment descriptor, and the following configuration illustrates the same:

```
<window>
    <window-name>CMS_Window</window-name>
    <content>
        <content-type>cms</content-type>
        <content-uri>/cms/index.html</content-uri>
    </content>
    <region>center</region>
    <height>1</height>
</window>
```

The windows initially loads the page indicated by `<content-uri>`. However, all subsequent navigation remains within the same portlet window.

CMS service configuration

As discussed earlier, JBoss portal uses Apache Jackrabbit to implement the content and repository management. Hence, the configuration of Content Management Portlet is pretty much the configuration of Jackrabbit configuration files.

The configuration for Jackrabbit can be found in the file `portal-cms.sar/META-INF-INF/jboss-service.xml`.

Although, there are a lot of options, most of the default settings work just fine. The following is a snippet indicating just how these options that can be tweaked:

```
<depends optional-attribute-name="StackFactory"
                    proxy-type="attribute">
```

```
portal:service=InterceptorStackFactory,type=Cms
</depends>
      <attribute name="DoChecking">true</attribute>
      <attribute name="DefaultContentLocation">
         portal/cms/conf/default-content/default/
      </attribute>
      <attribute name="DefaultLocale">en</attribute>
      <attribute name="RepositoryName">PortalRepository</attribute>
      <attribute name="HomeDir">
         ${jboss.server.data.dir}${/}portal${/}cms${/}conf
      </attribute>
   ...
</depends>
```

Each configuration option listed above can be defined as follows:

1. `DoChecking`: Indicates whether the portal should check the content repository configuration files and the default content

2. `DefaultContentLocation`: Location of the default content used to pre-populate the repository

3. `DefaultLocale`: Default language and locale; ISO-639 two-letter abbreviation

4. `RepositoryName`: A name for the repository

5. `HomeDir`: When content is stored entirely within the file system, this indicates the location of the configuration

Currently, the default prefix for content served from the repository is `content`, resulting in URLs such as `http://domain/content/test.html`. Any content that is accessed with `content` in the URL will trigger the portal to render the content. However, if we want to change the prefix value, we can edit the `portal-cms.sar/META-INF-INF/jboss-service.xml` file and update the "Prefix" option.

Content storage configuration

Content storage is an important part of the CMS. JBoss portal CMS, by default, stores all of its configurations, node properties, and references in the database. However, this value can also be changed based on the specific needs of applications.

The three types of content storage options are:

1. 100% database

2. 100% filesystem

3. Mixed

100% database storage

This is the default configuration and doesn't require any special configuration.

100% filesystem storage

As mentioned earlier, the portal server, by default, uses a database for storage. It uses **Hibernate** to interact with the database. To update the configuration for this, the `jboss-portal.sar/portal-cms.sar/META-INF/jboss-service.xml` file needs to be edited.

Updating the files is a four-step process, but the basic idea is to remove references to `HibernateStore` and the `HibernatePersistenceManager` classes, and substitute them with references to the `LocalFileSystem` and `XMLPersistenceManager` classes.

1. Comment out `HibernateStore` in three locations:

   ```
   <!-- HibernateStore: uses RDBMS + Hibernate for storage -->
   <FileSystem class="org.jboss.portal.cms.hibernate.HibernateStore">
   ...
   </FileSystem>
   ```

2. Uncomment the block under each one of them that enables the `LocalFilesystem` classes:

   ```
   <!-- LocalFileSystem: uses FileSystem for storage. -->
   <FileSystem class="org.apache.jackrabbit.core.fs.local.
                       LocalFileSystem">
   ...
   </FileSystem>
   ```

3. Comment out `HibernatePersistenceManager` in three locations:

   ```
   <!-- HibernatePersistentManager:
        uses RDBMS + Hibernate for storage -->
   <PersistenceManager class="org.jboss.portal.cms.hibernate.state.
                             HibernatePersistenceManager">
   ...
   </PersistenceManager>
   ```

4. Uncomment `XMLPersistenceManager` under the above references:

   ```
   <!-- XMLPersistenceManager: uses FileSystem for storage -->
   <PersistenceManager class="org.apache.jackrabbit.core.state.
                             xml.XMLPersistenceManager"/>
   ```

Mixed Storage

Mixed storage involves storing metadata in the database, but blobs in the file system. This type of storage is especially useful when storing large files or streaming media content.

Configuration is made in the `boss-portal.sar/portal-cms.sar/META-INF/jboss-service.xml` file, and involves changing an option from:

```
<param name="externalBLOBs" value="false"/>
```

to:

```
<param name="externalBLOBs" value="true"/>
```

CMS Interceptors

The CMS portlet uses some of the services, such as Interceptors, that are part of the overall CMS service.

Interceptors are another strong feature in the Portal CMS. By function, they serve as conduits for every request made for the portal, thus allowing them to introduce and execute certain functions before transferring control to the destination entity. They allow application developers to easily customize the behavior to fit the needs.

Interceptors can be created by extending the class `org.jboss.portal.cms.CMSInterceptor` and providing the content of the class `JCRCommand` method.

Interceptors are used by the server for various functions such as security, workflow, and so on. We will discuss workflows and their configuration in the next section.

Interceptors are added to the `portal-cms-sar/META-INF/jboss-service.xml` file, and the following snippet shows the entry for a security Interceptor:

```
<!-- ACL Security Interceptor -->
<mbean code="org.jboss.portal.cms.impl.interceptors.ACLInterceptor"
    name="portal:service=Interceptor,type=Cms,name=ACL" xmbean-dd=""
    xmbean-code="org.jboss.portal.jems.as.system.
                 JBossServiceModelMBean">
<xmbean />
<attribute name="JNDIName">
    java:/portal/cms/ACLInterceptor
</attribute>
<attribute name="CmsSessionFactory">
    java:/portal/cms/CMSSessionFactory
</attribute>
```

```
            <attribute name="IdentitySessionFactory">
               java:/portal/IdentitySessionFactory
            </attribute>
            <attribute name="DefaultPolicy">
               <policy>
                  <!-- permissions on the root cms node -->
                  <criteria name="path" value="/">
                     <permission name="cms" action="read">
                        <role name="Anonymous" />
                     </permission>
                        permission name="cms" action="write">
                        <role name="User" />
                     </permission>
                     <permission name="cms" action="manage">
                        <role name="Admin" />
                     </permission>
                  </criteria>
                  <!-- permissions on the default cms node -->
                  <criteria name="path" value="/default">
                     <permission name="cms" action="read">
                        <role name="Anonymous" />
                     </permission>
                     <permission name="cms" action="write">
                        <role name="User" />
                     </permission>
                     <permission name="cms" action="manage">
                        <role name="Admin" />
                     </permission>
                  </criteria>
                  <!-- permissions on the private/protected node -->
                  <criteria name="path" value="/default/private">
                     <permission name="cms" action="manage">
                        <role name="Admin" />
                     </permission>
                  </criteria>
               </policy>
            </attribute>
            <depends optional-attribute-name="AuthorizationManager"
               proxy-type="attribute">
               portal:service=AuthorizationManager,type=cms
            </depends>
            <depends>portal:service=Hibernate,type=CMS</depends>
            <depends>
               portal:service=Module,type=IdentityServiceController
            </depends>
         </mbean>
```

An example configuration for a custom interceptor that has been created is as follows:

```
<mbean code="org.example.CMSInterceptor"
       name="portal:service=Interceptor,type=Cms,name=CMSName"
       xmbean-dd=""
       xmbean-code="org.jboss.portal.common.system.
                    JBossServiceModelMBean">
   <xmbean />
</mbean>
```

Localization

The CMS Portlet provides localization support as mentioned earlier. The two-letter abbreviations of ISO-639 are supported, and the portlet first checks for the preferred locale, typically set in the browser, before it serves content based on the default value.

CMS workflow service

We briefly made reference to the approval process and workflow for publishing content, but we never really went into detail. Let us dig a bit deeper into the CMS approval process that can be triggered for every content update and creation.

The CMS approval process is an optional configuration option that can be turned on to introduce a publication approval workflow for any type of content that is newly created, or any existing content that is updated, before it goes live. The process, in general, adds the change requests to a queue, and waits for an assigned role to approve or deny the change for publication to the live web site.

Activation and configuration

JBoss portal uses JBoss jBPM, workflow engine to implement its CMS workflow features. jBPM is a powerful, feature-rich business process and workflow tool which provides a large number of options for granular control of content workflow

Activating the approval workflow is as simple as uncommenting some lines in the portal configuration file `jboss-portal.sar/portal-cms.sar/META-INF/jboss-service.xml`.

In the Mbean `org.jboss.portal.cms.impl.jcr.JCRCMS` file, we need to uncomment the section that has an attribute name of `ApprovePublishWorkflow`.

The following code snippet illustrates the edit:

```
<mbean code="org.jboss.portal.cms.impl.jcr.JCRCMS"
    name="portal:service=CMS" xmbean-dd=""
    xmbean-code="org.jboss.portal.jems.as.system.
               JBossServiceModelMBean">
    <xmbean />
    ...
    <!-- publish/approval workflow integration -->
    <depends optional-attribute-name="ApprovePublishWorkflow"
                            proxy-type="attribute">
        portal:service=ApprovePublish,type=Workflow
    </depends>
    ...
</mbean>
```

The above change will activate the workflow feature. However, to configure and customize the service, we need to edit another file. This time, it will be the `jboss-portal.sar/portal-workflow.sar/META-INF/jboss-service.xml` file.

This file has many options for tweaking and customizing the service. The following is a snippet of the file, which illustrates the various configuration options available.

```
<!-- ApprovePublish workflow service -->
<mbean code="org.jboss.portal.workflow.cms.ApprovePublishImpl"
    name="portal:service=ApprovePublish,type=Workflow" xmbean-dd=""
    xmbean-code="org.jboss.portal.jems.as.system.
               JBossServiceModelMBean">
    <xmbean></xmbean>
    <depends optional-attribute-name="WorkflowService"
                            proxy-type="attribute">
        portal:service=Workflow,type=WorkflowService
    </depends>
    <!-- JBPM process definition -->
    <attribute name="Process">
        <![CDATA[
                <!-- cms approval workflow -->
                    <process-definition name="approval_workflow">
                <start-state>
                    <transition to="request_approval"></transition>
                </start-state>
                  <task-node name="request_approval" signal="first">
                    <task name="approve_publish">
                        <assignment class="org.jboss.portal.core.
                            workflow.cms.PublishAssignmentHandler">
                        </assignment>
                        <event type="task-start">
                            <action class="org.jboss.portal.cms.
                                workflow.FinalizePublish">
```

```
                    </action>
                </event>
                <exception-handler>
                    <action class="org.jboss.portal.workflow.
                                   cms.TaskExceptionHandler">
                    </action>
                </exception-handler>
              </task>
              <transition name="approval" to="end">
              </transition>
              <transition name="rejection" to="end">
              </transition>
            </task-node>
            <end-state name="end"></end-state>
          </process-definition>
        \]\]\>
      </attribute>
  ...

      <!--
         a comma separated list of portal roles that are
         designated to act as workflow managers. They are
         allowed to approve/reject content publish requests
      -->
      <attribute name="ManagerRoles">Admin</attribute>
      <attribute name="JNDIName">
          java:portal/ApprovePublishWorkflow
      </attribute>
  </mbean>
```

The salient configuration options, as seen in the preceding configuration file, are the JBPM configuration and manager roles.

Summary

JBoss portal provides a simple but robust content management system that is sufficient for most of the needs of a portal application. Using Interceptors, CMSAdmin, and CMS Portlets, developers can provide functionality that effectively helps to manage and deliver content.

We extended our example further to add some new content, and then edited this content. We saw how easy it is to add, edit, and manage content on the portal. The portal also provides customizable workflow and localization capabilities

In the next chapter, we will discuss another important aspect of portal usage—portal security and access rights management.

9
Portal Security

The features and functionality provided by portals and portlets are a lot more effective in enterprise environments when they are accompanied by fine-grained access controls and security. Portals provide personalized access to content, applications, and functionality. Hence, security has to be custom tailored to meet the needs of the users, while providing a secure functional platform.

Security in JBoss portal includes user authentication and authorization, portlet security, encryption support, management of users and controls, and WebServices security for remote portlets.

In this chapter, we will discuss each one of these options, illustrate the steps for configuring them, and review some of the best practices for ensuring a secure portal environment.

Portal security

User security and content security form the core of any security configuration on the JBoss portal. Tied to user security aspects such as authentication and authorization are features such as single sign-on, LDAP configuration, identity management, and so on. Content security can be categorized under portlets, portal pages, portal server, managed content, and so on.

In addition to portal-specific aspects, a portal-based application also has to deal with traditional security issues related to application vulnerabilities, including SQL injection, cross-site scripting and so on.

Authentication and authorization form the basis of user security and access control in applications. Authentication tells us "who you are", while authorization tells us "what you can do". Both authentication and authorization use a combination of enterprise registries such as LDAP server, and custom code for user information validation and access control.

In the next few sections, we will talk about each of the above aspects, as they relate to portal security, in detail. Starting with the security of portal objects, we will explore user security configuration, and eventually talk about user identity management.

Portal objects security

Portal instances, portlet instances, and portal pages are all examples of portal objects that can be secured in JBoss portal. These objects can be secured using both configuration and management portlets provided by the console.

Using the management console

To configure portal object security using the management console, we need to log in to the portal console as **admin** and access the **Admin** section of the console page.

The first portal objects that we want to look at securing are the portal instances. The server provides options to control the security constraints of a portal instance, thereby allowing us granular control of the portal application at the highest level.

Portal instances are configured from the admin console of the server. As shown in the following screenshot, once we access the **Admin** section, we are, by default, presented with the portal instance management screen:

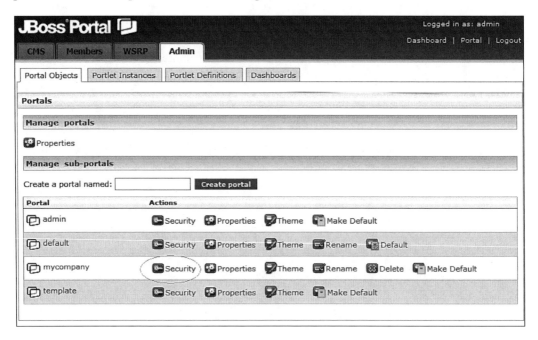

After clicking on the **Security** link, we will see the options to set various permissions for a given set of roles, as shown in the following screenshot:

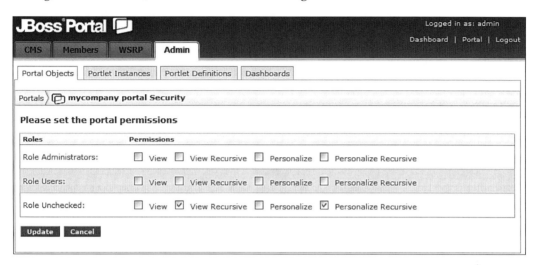

Here, the current security configuration states that for a **Role Unchecked**, access should be allowed to view the node and all of the child nodes and elements of the portal node. **Unchecked** is a special role that indicates "everybody". **View Recursive** implies allowing view access recursively to all of the child nodes and elements.

The second type of objects that we might want to manage are the portal pages. From the same admin pages, once we drill down further into a particular portal of our choice, we can see all of the pages in the portal. Clicking on the security tab for each page provides us with a screen with portal page security constraints, as shown in the example following:

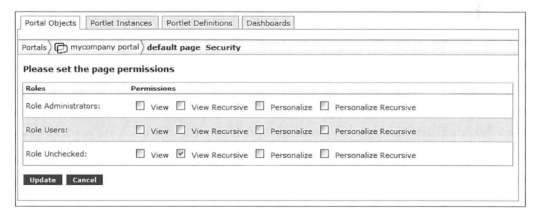

We can again control the permissions for the page, for a given set of roles, by selecting or deselecting checkboxes. Selecting the **View** box next to, say, **Role Users**, will give everyone who belongs to the **Role Users** view access to the default page.

Our next portal objects are portlets, and they can be similarly secured from the management console by using the **Portlet Instances** tab. The following screenshot shows the security setting for a portlet instance:

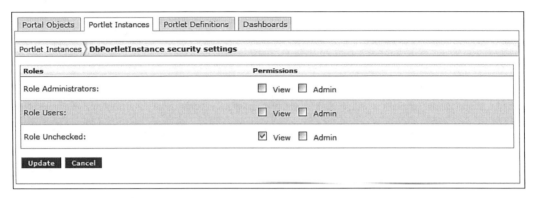

Although the management console offers an easy way to configure the security constraints in the portal, it is sometimes a lot more convenient (and consistent) to configure these settings in the application by using configuration files. Let's see how we can configure the same elements we have just seen using the configuration files.

Using configuration files

We have just seen how the security constraints can be set by using the JBoss portal server console. The same settings can also be configured in the portlet configuration files. The following example demonstrates the security setting for a portal page named, `mycompany.default`:

Portal objects can be secured using either the JBoss Portal `*-object.xml` descriptor or the `portlet-instances.xml` descriptor.

The security and action are defined in the node `<security-constraint>` as follows:

```
<?xml version="1.0" encoding="UTF-8"?>
<deployments>
   <deployment>
      <if-exists>overwrite</if-exists>
      <parent-ref>mycompany</parent-ref>
    <page>
      <page-name>default</page-name>
```

```
<security-constraint>
    <policy-permission>
        <action-name>view</action-name>
        <role-name>SPECIAL_USER</role-name>
    </policy-permission>
</security-constraint>
 <window>
    <window-name>ViewPortletWindow</window-name>
    <instance-ref>ViewPortletInstance</instance-ref>
    <region>right</region>
    <height>1</height>
 </window>
 <properties>
        . .
 </properties>
 </page>
</deployment>
. .
<deployments>
```

This example grants everyone a privilege to view the current object and any child object recursively. The `<unchecked />` tag specifies that the assignment can be for anyone, also called an unchecked role.

Access rights

- `view`: Users can view the page
- `viewrecursive`: Users can view the page and any child pages of that page
- `personalize`: Users are able to personalize the page's theme, layouts and so on
- `personalizerecursive`: Users are able to personalize the page AND the children pages' themes

Role Definition

- `<unchecked/>`: Anyone can view this page
- `<role-name>SPECIAL_USER</role-name>`: Access to this page is limited to the defined role

If you recall the screen we saw earlier that showed the security constraints for the default page on the admin console, you will remember that it gave **View Recursive** access to everybody.

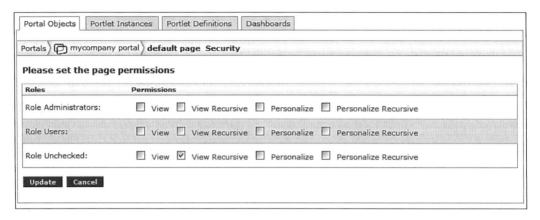

Once deployed, the new configuration of the page changes to provide different constraints, granting only **View** access to the new role of **SPECIAL_USER**.

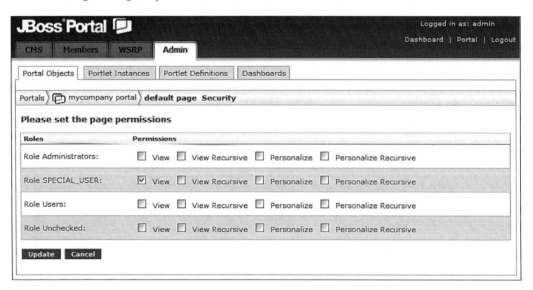

Similar to the management console, portal objects, such as portal instances, portlets, and portal pages, can be individually configured by adding the `<security-constraint>` tag to the `portlet-instances.xml` file or the `*-object.xml` file. The role definition and the access rights remain the same.

We have just seen the configuration for the portal page. Let us look at the configuration of the other objects.

For example, to configure security on a portal instance, the `mycompany-object.xml` is configured as follows:

```
<deployment>
    <parent-ref />
    <if-exists>overwrite</if-exists>
    <portal>
        <portal-name>mycompany</portal-name>
        <supported-modes>
            <mode>view</mode>
        </supported-modes>
        <supported-window-states>
            <window-state>normal</window-state>
        </supported-window-states>
        <properties>
            ..
        </properties>
        <security-constraint>
            <policy-permission>
                <action-name>personalizerecursive</action-name>
                <unchecked />
            </policy-permission>
            <policy-permission>
                <action-name>personalizerecursive</action-name>
                <<role-name>SPECIAL_USER</role-name>
            </policy-permission>
        </security-constraint>
        <page>
            <page-name>default</page-name>
            <window>
                ..
            </window>
        </page>
    </portal>
</deployment>
```

Portal pages can be similarly configured in the `mycompany-object.xml` file, as shown:

```
<?xml version="1.0" encoding="UTF-8"?>
<deployments>
    <deployment>
        <if-exists>overwrite</if-exists>
```

```
        <parent-ref>mycompany</parent-ref>
    <page>
    <page-name>default</page-name>
    <security-constraint>
        <policy-permission>
            <action-name>view</action-name>
            <role-name>SPECIAL_USER</role-name>
        </policy-permission>
    </security-constraint>
     <window>
        <window-name>ViewPortletWindow</window-name>
        <instance-ref>ViewPortletInstance</instance-ref>
        <region>right</region>
        <height>1</height>
     </window>
     <properties>
            <property>
        <name>layout.id</name>
        <value>mycompany_threecol</value>
            </property>
        <property>
        <name>theme.id</name>
        <value>mycompany_theme</value>
            </property>
            <property>
        <name>theme.renderSetId</name>
        <value>mycompany_divRenderer</value>
            </property>
     </properties>
      </page>
     </deployment>

 ..
</deployments>
```

As we can see the, the explicit `<page>` element is used to configure constraints on a specific portal page named `default`.

Security constraints on the portlet can be configured in the `portal-instance.xml` file, and this configuration appears as follows:

```
<?xml version="1.0" standalone="yes"?>
<deployments>
    ..
    <deployment>
        <instance>
```

```
        <instance-id>DbPortletInstance</instance-id>
        <portlet-ref>DbPortlet</portlet-ref>
    <security-constraint>
    <policy-permission>
        <action-name>view</action-name>
        <role-name>SPECIAL_USER</role-name>
    </policy-permission>
    </security-constraint>
    </instance>
  </deployment>
</deployments>
```

We can see that the security constraints can be applied to the portal objects at a pretty fine-grained level of detail, using both the admin console as well as the configuration files.

As applications become complex, constraint definitions tend to be become very important, complex, and an integral part of the portal applications.

User security and access control

Until now, we have been talking about securing assets. However, as we have seen in the constraint declaration, every asset is restricted to a certain role, and every role ties back to a user or an entity. In this segment, we will discuss the ways in which authentication and authorization is facilitated in JBoss portal. We will also discuss other aspects related to authentication and user management, such as single sign-on and identity management. Identity management, in our case, is the process of facilitating the management of users and attributes such as passwords, roles, and so on.

Authentication

Authentication in JBoss portal builds on the JEE security provided by the JBoss server. The JEE specification defines the roles and constraints under which certain URLs and components are protected. However, this might not always be sufficient for building enterprise applications or portals. Application server providers such as JBoss supplement the authentication and authorization features provided by the JEE specification with additional features such as role-to-group mapping and session logout.

Authentication in JBoss portal can be divided into configuration files and portal server configuration.

The jboss-portal.sar/portal-server.war file is the portal deployment on the JBoss application server. Assuming that the portal server is like any JEE application deployed on an application server, all user authentication configurations go into the WEB-INF/web.xml and the WEB-INF/jboss-web.xml files.

1. The WEB-INF/web.xml entry defines the authentication mode, with the default being form-based authentication. This file is also used to define the login and error pages, as defined by the JEE specification.

2. The default security domain defined by the JBoss application server is java:/jaas/portal for JBoss portal. The security domain maps the JEE security constructs to the operational domain. This is defined in a proprietary file, WEB-INF/jboss-web.xml. The portal security domain authentication stack is defined in the jboss-portal.sar/conf/login-config.xml file, and is deployed along with the portal. Login-config.xml houses the JAAS modules for authentication. Custom modules can be written and added here to support special scenarios. The server provides a defined set of JAAS login modules that can be used for various scenarios. For example, the IdentityLoginModule is used for authentication based on local portal data, SynchronizingLdapLoginModule for authentication using LDAP, and DBIdentityLoginModule for authentication using a database.

Within the jboss-portal.sar/portal-server.war application, all portal requests are routed through a single servlet called org.jboss.portal.server.servlet.PortalServlet. This servlet is defined twice, as follows, in the configuration file WEB-INF/web.xml to ensure that all possible request sources are covered:

*   PortalServletWithPathMapping for path mappings
*   PortalServletWithDefaultServletMapping for the default servlet mapping

The servlet is mapped four times with variations to address a combination of secure SSL access and authenticated URLs, as follows:

*   /*: Default access, and with no security constraint, allows access to everybody
*   /sec/*: All requests to a secure protocol are routed through this path, ensuring SSL transport
*   /auth/*: Authenticated access. Requires user to be authenticated before accessing the content under this tree
*   /authsec/*: An authenticated and secure access

The following snippet from `web.xml` shows the entries:

```
<!-- Provide access to unauthenticated users -->
<servlet-mapping>
    <servlet-name>PortalServletWithPathMapping</servlet-name>
    <url-pattern>/*</url-pattern>
</servlet-mapping>
<!-- Provide secure access to unauthenticated users -->
<servlet-mapping>
    <servlet-name>PortalServletWithPathMapping</servlet-name>
    <url-pattern>/sec/*</url-pattern>
</servlet-mapping>
<!-- Provide access to authenticated users -->
<servlet-mapping>
    <servlet-name>PortalServletWithPathMapping</servlet-name>
    <url-pattern>/auth/*</url-pattern>
</servlet-mapping>
<!-- Provide secure access to authenticated users -->
<servlet-mapping>
    <servlet-name>PortalServletWithPathMapping</servlet-name>
    <url-pattern>/authsec/*</url-pattern>
</servlet-mapping>
```

The URL patterns can be changed based on personal preference.

Authorization

Authorization is the process of determining if an authenticated user has access to a particular resource. Similar to authentication, JBoss portal provides in-built support for authorization, through **Java Authorization Contract for Containers (JACC)**. JACC is a JSR-115 specification for the authorization models of the Java2 and JEE enterprise platforms. In the next few sections, we will look at how JBoss portal facilitates authorization using JACC. However, before we go into the details of access controls and authorization configurations, let's quickly look at how roles are configured in JBoss Portal.

User and role management

A role is an authorization construct that denotes the group that a user of the portal belongs to. Typically, roles are used to determine the access rights and the extent of these rights for a given resource. We saw in an earlier section how we configured portal assets such as, portals, pages, and portlet instances, to restrict certain actions to specific roles. We used a role called **SPECIAL_USER** for our examples. However, we never really defined what this role means to JBoss portal.

Let's use the JBoss portal server console to register this role with the server.

Log in as **admin**, and then click on the **Members** tab. This takes us to the **User Management** and **Role Management** tabs.

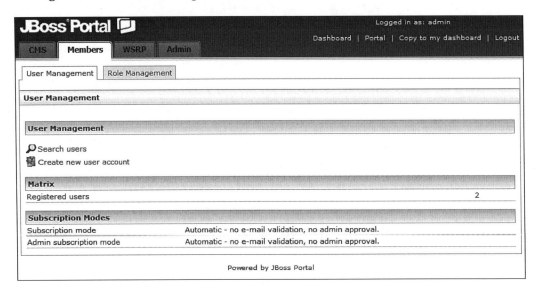

The **User Management** tab is used for creating new users. We will come back to this shortly, but for now, let's switch over to the **Role Management** tab and click on the **Create role** link on the bottom right of the page. We can now add our **SPECIAL_USER** role and provide a display name for it. Once we submit it, the role will be registered with the portal server.

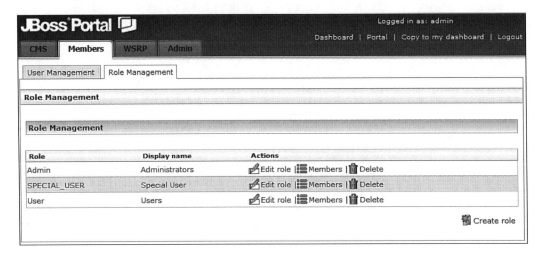

As we will see later, every attempt by an authenticated user to access a resource that has security constraints through a specific role will be matched by the portal before granting or denying access to the resource.

Users can be added to a role by using the **User Management** tab. Each user has a role property assigned, and this can be edited to check all of the roles that we want the user to belong to. We can see that for the user **User**, we now have an option to add the user to the **Special User** role.

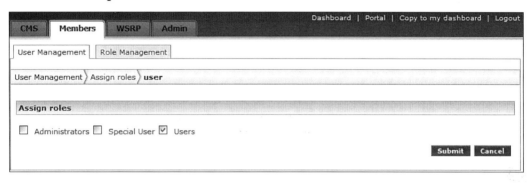

The portal permission

A permission object carries the relevant permission for a given entity. The `org.jboss.portal.security.PortalPermission` object is used to describe permission for the portal. Like all the other entity-specific permission classes, it extends the `java.security.Permission` class, and any permission checked in the portal should extend the `PortalPermission` as well. Two additional fields of significance are as follows:

- `uri`: A string that specifies the URI of the resource that is described by the permission

- `collection`: An object of class `org.jboss.portal.security.PortalPermissionCollection`, which is used when the permission acts as a container for other permissions

The authorization provider

The authorization provider is a generic interface of the type `org.jboss.portal.security.spi.provider.AuthorizationDomain`, and provides access to several services.

```
public interface AuthorizationDomain
{
    String getType();
```

```
    DomainConfigurator getConfigurator();
    PermissionRepository getPermissionRepository();
    PermissionFactory getPermissionFactory();
}
```

Let us look into these classes a bit more in detail:

- `org.jboss.portal.security.spi.provider.DomainConfigurator` provides configuration access to an authorization domain. The authorization schema consists of bindings between URIs, roles, and permissions.

- `org.jboss.portal.security.spi.provider.PermissionRepository` provides runtime access to the authorization domain. It is used to retrieve the permissions for a specific role and URI. It is used at runtime by the framework, to take security decisions.

- `org.jboss.portal.security.spi.provider.PermissionFactory` is a factory to instantiate permissions for the specific domain. It is used at runtime to create permission objects of the appropriate type by the security framework.

Making a programmatic security check

With this understanding of the background of the configuration files and the appropriate authorization API, we are now ready to make a programmatic security check. All we have to do is to create a permission of the correct type and check this against the `org.jboss.portal.spi.auth.PortalAuthorizationManager` service. This service is used internally by JBoss server and is connected to the various authorization providers, for a runtime decision based on the type of permission. Access to this service is through `org.jboss.portal.spi.auth.PortalAuthorizationManagerFactory`. The factory is a portal service that is usually added to services as follows:

```xml
<?xml version="1.0" encoding="UTF-8"?>
<server>
  ...
  <mbean
     code='MyService"
     name="portal:service=MyService">
    <depends
       optional-attribute-name="PortalAuthorizationManagerFactory"
       proxy-type="attribute">
         portal:service=PortalAuthorizationManagerFactory
    </depends>
    ...
  </mbean>
  ...
</server>
```

It can be added to the servlet context of a WAR file in the `WEB-INF/jboss-portlet.xml` file, as follows:

```
<?xml version="1.0" encoding="UTF-8"?>
<!DOCTYPE portlet-app PUBLIC
    "-//JBoss Portal//DTD JBoss Portlet 3.0//EN"
    "http://www.jboss.org/portal/dtd/jboss-portlet_3.0.dtd">
<portlet-app>
    ...
    <service>
        <service-name>PortalAuthorizationManagerFactory</service-name>
        <service-class>
        org.jboss.portal.security.spi.auth.
PortalAuthorizationManagerFactory
        </service-class>
        <service-ref>:service=PortalAuthorizationManagerFactory</
service-ref>
    </service>
    ...
</portlet-app>
```

Here is an example of how a security check is made for a specific page:

```
PortalAuthorizationManager pam = factory.getManager();
PortalObjectId id = page.getId();
PortalObjectPermission perm = new PortalObjectPermission(id,
PortalObjectPermission.VIEW_MASK);
if (pam.checkPermission(perm) == false)
{
    System.out.println("Current user is not authorized to view page " +
id);
}
```

Configuring an authorization domain

Configuring a domain can be done through the `DomainConfigurator` interface:

```
public interface DomainConfigurator
{
    Set getSecurityBindings(String uri);
    void setSecurityBindings(String uri, Set securityBindings)
            throws SecurityConfigurationException;
    void removeSecurityBindings(String uri)
            throws SecurityConfigurationException;
}
```

The various methods of this interface allow configuration of security bindings for a given resource, where a resource is naturally identified by a URI. The `org.jboss.portal.security.RoleSecurityBinding` object is an object that encapsulates a role name and a set of actions bound to this role.

```
RoleSecurityBinding binding1 = new RoleSecurityBinding(Collections.
singleton("view"), "Admin");
RoleSecurityBinding binding2 = new RoleSecurityBinding(Collections.
singleton("view"), "User");
Set bindings = new HashSet();
bindings.add(binding1);
bindings.add(binding2);
configurator.setSecurityBinding(pageURI, bindings);
```

LDAP configuration

Light-weight Directory Access Protocol (LDAP) is an important component of an enterprise portal architecture. Due to its specialized nature, it is usually the repository of all user information, including user IDs/passwords and roles.

LDAP support can be enabled through the following steps:

1. **Configure LDAP properties on the server**. LDAP can be configured in JBoss portal in two ways. We can either change the `IdentityServiceController` section of the portal service configuration file `jboss-service.xml` to point to a different identity file, or we can leave the configuration intact and change the identity file.

    Let's look at these options in detail:

    Let's open the file `$JBOSS_HOME/server/default/deploy/jboss-portal.sar/META-INF/jboss-service.xml`.

    Change the `ConfigFile` option to `ldap-identity-config.xml`; this file comes with the portal server and can be found in the `conf/` directory.

    ```
    <mbean
        code="org.jboss.portal.identity.IdentityServiceControllerImpl"
        name="portal:service=Module,type=IdentityServiceController"
        xmbean-dd=""
        xmbean-code="org.jboss.portal.jems.as.system.
                    JBossServiceModelMBean">
        <xmbean/>
        <depends>portal:service=Hibernate</depends>
        <attribute name="JndiName">
            java:/portal/IdentityServiceController
        </attribute>
    ```

```
<attribute name="RegisterMBeans">true</attribute>
<attribute name="ConfigFile">
   conf/identity/identity-config.xml
</attribute>
<attribute name="DefaultConfigFile">
   conf/identity/standardidentity-config.xml
</attribute>
</mbean>
```

Alternatively, we can swap the contents of the identity-config.xml and ldap_dentity-config.xml files.

2. **Set up an LDAP Connection**. After identifying the appropriate configuration file for identity management, we can now configure LDAP properties and connections in the file, ldap_identity-config.xml (or identity-config.xml, depending on the approach chosen above).

An LDAP tree appears as follows. It has clearly defined groups, users, and their names organized in a tree form. A typical LDAP interaction process involves connecting to the LDAP server and then looking up a user by using the tree structure.

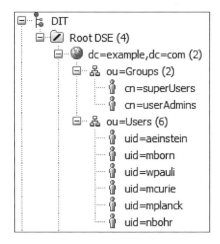

Our configuration file to connect to the LDAP server will look like this:

```
<datasource>
    <name>LDAP</name>
    <config>
        <option>
            <name>host</name>
            <value>localhost</value>
        </option>
```

```
        <option>
            <name>port</name>
            <value>10389</value>
        </option>
        <option>
            <name>adminDN</name>
            <value> uid=admin,ou=system </value>
        </option>
        <option>
            <name>adminPassword</name>
            <value>abc123</value>
        </option>
    </config>
</datasource>
```

We are now connected to the LDAP server; all subsequent requests for authentication will now be routed to this server.

So, the user **wpauli** will have the following information stored for him in the LDAP tree. After authentication, we can also get the other details of the user.

Attribute Description	Value
objectClass	*inetOrgPerson (structural)*
objectClass	*organizationalPerson (structural)*
objectClass	*person (structural)*
objectClass	*top (abstract)*
objectClass	*uidObject (auxiliary)*
cn	Wolfgang Pauli
sn	Pauli
uid	wpauli
facsimiletelephonenumber	+1 904 982 6883
givenname	Wolfgang
mail	wpauli@example.com
ou	Users
roomnumber	667
telephonenumber	+1 904 982 6882
userpassword	Plain text password

Apart from these, there are few other LDAP features provided by the server, such as connection pooling, SSL-based access, tree management, and so on, that can facilitate a productive interaction with an LDAP server.

Single sign-on

Single Sign-On, or **SSO**, is a process in which the user logs into the system only once, and all his or her future interaction with any subsequent systems is seamless and doesn't require the user to be authenticated over and over again for each system. Portlets within a portal server integrate seamlessly as the user credentials are transferred easily within the system, but the same is not true for systems that are outside of the portal server, on the intranet or on the Internet.

JBoss portal offers support for various SSO packages in the industry that help to provide seamless integration between various functionalities and systems.

We will consider the **Central Authentication Service (CAS)** as our SSO provider, and we need to make sure that we have both the server and client CAS binaries, along with the deployable WAR file, with us before we start the integration. The binaries can be found on the CAS web site at `http://www.ja-sig.org/products/cas/downloads/index.html`.

The following steps walk us through the configuration and integration of CAS with JBoss portal server:

1. Open the `cas.war` file provided by the CAS project, and copy the `portal-identity-lib.jar` and `portal-identity-sso-lib.jar` files. Please note that the WAR file can have a different name based on the release. Copy the file from `$JBOSS_HOME/server/default/deploy/jboss-portal.sar/lib` to `$JBOSS_HOME/server/default/deploy/cas.war/WEB-INF/lib`.

2. Uncomment the following entry in the file `$JBOSS_HOME/server/default/deploy/jboss-portal.sar/portal-server.war/WEB-INF/context.xml`. This configures the `login`, `logout`, and `validate` pages when requests for these actions are made on the portal.

```
<Valve
className="org.jboss.portal.identity.sso.cas.
                    CASAuthenticationValve"
    casLogin="https://localhost:8080/cas/login"
    casLogout="https://localhost:8080/cas/logout"
    casValidate="https://localhost:8080/cas-server-webapp-
                3.3.1/serviceValidate"
    casServerName="localhost:8080"
    authType="FORM"
/>
```

The ports and the server name should be changed based on the local configuration. Please note that CAS requires SSL to function effectively. Hence, it might be a good idea to enable SSL on the JBoss server. You can find more details at `http://www.jboss.org/jbossas/docs/`.

3. Add the `casclient.jar` library to the portal project. The client JAR can be found at `http://repository.jboss.com/cas/3.0.7/lib/`.

4. Uncomment the following lines in the `$JBOSS_HOME/server/default/deploy/jboss-portal.sar/META-INF/jboss-service.xml` file. This notifies the portal server that all authentication-related requests need to be directed to CAS.

```
<mbean
    code="org.jboss.portal.identity.sso.cas.
                    CASAuthenticationService"
    name="portal:service=Module,type=CASAuthenticationService"
    xmbean-dd=""
    xmbean-code="org.jboss.portal.jems.as.system
                    .JBossServiceModelMBean">
    <xmbean/>
    <depends>
        portal:service=Module,type=IdentityServiceController
    </depends>
    <attribute name="HavingRole"></attribute>
</mbean>
```

5. So far, we have been creating interfaces for use by CAS `AuthenticationHandler`. We will now create the `authenticationHandler` instance in CAS, which will use the service that we created earlier in the JBoss server. Edit the `$JBOSS_HOME/server/default/deploy/cas.war/WEB-INF/deployerConfigContext.xml` file, and replace the following line in the `authenticationHandlers` section:

```
<bean class="org.jasig.cas.authentication.handler.support.
            SimpleTestUsernamePasswordAuthenticationHandler" />
```

with the following line:

```
<bean class="org.jboss.portal.identity.sso.cas.
            CASAuthenticationHandler" />
```

A good test to verify the installation and configuration of CAS is to go to the portal home page and click on the **Login** link. IF CAS is installed successfully, the **Login** page should now be a **CAS authentication server** login page, overriding the default JBoss portal login page.

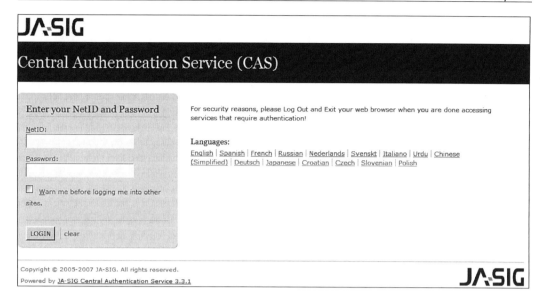

Once authenticated, CAS will hand over the control back to the application and pass the user credentials.

Identity management

Identity management is dealing with issues such as provisioning of users, user profile, lost passwords, password resets, and so on, for the portal platform.

Identity in JBoss portal can be managed in a couple of ways:

- **Using Identity Portlets**: For most scenarios, this is the one that you are most likely to use.
- **Using Identity Management API**: This is largely used for advanced configurations and added flexibility.

Managing users using admin console

One of the easiest ways to manage users is to use the JBoss portal server admin console. We talked about this before when we talked about role management.

To use this, we go back to the **Members** tab of the admin console, when we are logged in as **admin**.

In the **User Management** tab, we can create users; once they are created, we can assign them to the role.

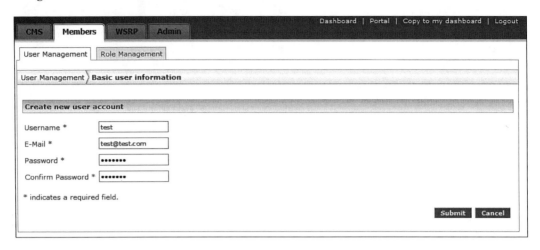

Obviously, this method can only be used when an administrator is creating new accounts. In portals, users often prefer to create their own accounts. Let's see how we can do that.

Identity portlets

The identity portlets are a set of portlets provided by default in JBoss portal, and for the most part provide UI-based management of user information and general identity management. The identity portlets provided by JBoss portal are as follows:

- **The User Portlet**: This deals with all user-related actions, such as lost/reset password, profile changes, CAPTCHA support, and so on.

- **The Identity Management Portlet**: This deals with user-role mapping and management.

The identity portlets together support security features such as CAPTCHAs, user provisioning including lost passwords, and password resets, and business process-based user registration using jBPM.

Captcha support

CAPTCHA has lately become a very popular approach for web applications to identify and isolate human users versus automated bots. This is specifically useful from a security perspective. All of us have seen examples of a CAPTCHA when we register on an Internet web site, or add comments on postings. A CAPTCHA is the oddly-distorted images of characters and numerals that we read and manually enter in a provided text area. The idea is to force manual reading and entry, which automatically prevents automated bots from registering or posting. **CAPTCHA is an acronym for Completely Automated Public Turing test to tell Computers and Humans Apart**. **JCaptcha** is an open source project that offers a Java-based implementation of CAPTCHA. JBoss portal's user portlet leverages JCaptcha to provide a challenge-response feature in JBoss portal for user registration.

The following figure illustrates the JBoss registration screen and the offered CAPTCH image:

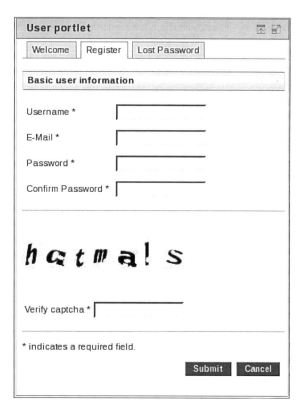

CAPTCHA is not enabled by default, and changing the portlet preference `captcha` to `true` enables CAPTCHA for user registration and lost password management.

```
...
<portlet>
...
    <display-name>User portlet</display-name>
...
    <portlet-preferences>
        <preference>
            <name>captcha</name>
            <value>true</value>
        </preference>
    </portlet-preferences>
</portlet>
...
```

Lost and reset passwords

The user management portlet provides the lost password feature in which the password is reset after the user provides username. The following example shows entry enabling the lost password feature.

```
...
<portlet>
...
    <display-name>User portlet</display-name>
...
    <portlet-preferences>
        <preference>
            <name>lostPassword</name>
            <value>true</value>
        </preference>
    </portlet-preferences>
</portlet>
...
```

Both the lost function and the reset function are offered by the portlet. However, the process changes slightly when the user chooses to reset their password, as opposed to requesting a lost password. For the reset password feature, the password of the user is changed to a random value and will be sent to the user's email address.

```
...
<portlet>
...
```

```
    <display-name>User management portlet</display-name>
...
    <portlet-preferences>
          <preference>
                  <name>resetPassword</name>
                  <value>true</value>
          </preference>
    </portlet-preferences>
</portlet>
..
```

jBPM-based user registration

JBoss portal leverages jBPM to supplement user registration with workflow support. **jBPM** or **Java Business Process Management**, is an open source J2EE-based workflow management system. Among other things, it helps to facilitate the flow of a process, involving various tasks and checkpoints involving users and actions. A user registration process is quite similar. Using jBPM as a workflow engine, the idea is to provide features that allow efficient moderation and confirmation of the registration process. By default, JBoss portal provides three different subscription modes:

1. **Automatic subscription**, where there is no business process involved and the user can directly log in after registration.

2. **E-Mail validation**, where the user verifies the registration by clicking on a link in an email. The email is generated by the portal server using jBPM.

3. **E-Mail validation and admin approval**, where the user is validated not only through email, but also approved by the portal administrator.

Configuration

There are a few levers and configurations that JBoss portal provides to configure the portlets. The configuration file is `jboss-portal.sar/portal-identity.sar/conf/identity-ui-configuration.xml`.

A sample configuration is as follows:

```
<identity-ui-configuration>
    <subscription-mode>automatic</subscription-mode>
    <admin-subscription-mode>automatic</admin-subscription-mode>
    <overwrite-workflow>false</overwrite-workflow>
    <email-domain>jboss.org</email-domain>
    <email-from>no-reply@jboss.com</email-from>
    <password-generation-characters>
        a...Z
```

```
    </password-generation-characters>
    <default-roles>
        <role>User</role>
    </default-roles>
    <!-- user interface components -->
    <ui-components>
    <ui-component name="givenname">
         <property-ref>user.name.given</property-ref>
       </ui-component>
       <ui-component name="familyname">
          <property-ref>user.name.family</property-ref>
       </ui-component>
       ...
</identity-ui-configuration>
```

Identity management API

The identity management API is used for fine-grained control of user-related features, and to manually configure specialized sources of user data such as LDAP servers, RDBMS databases, and so on. We talked earlier about users, roles, and their relationships. We used the administration console to establish the relationships. The identity API helps build such solutions programmatically for custom needs when the user and the role information come from external sources.

The various interfaces provided are as follows:

- The org.jboss.portal.identity.User interface represents a user and provides operations for managing user attributes

- The org.jboss.portal.identity.Role interface represents a Role and provides operations to manage user role

- The org.jboss.portal.identity.UserModule interface exposes operations for users management

- The org.jboss.portal.identity.RoleModule interface exposes operations for role management

- The MembershipModule interface exposes operations for obtaining or managing relationships between users and roles

- The UserProfileModule interface exposes operations to access and manage information stored in a user profile

- The `ProfileInfo` interface can be obtained by using the `UserProfileModule`, and exposes meta information of a profile

- `PropertyInfo` interface expose methods to obtain information about accessible properties in a user profile

Any of the above interfaces can be used and configured to provide fine-grained control of assets. The configurations can be found in `jboss-portal.sar/conf/identity/identity-config.xml`.

Content management system security

The JBoss portal CMS is a combination of folders and files. All such assets can be effectively secured using a combination of users and roles. The permissions here relate to the content on the portal, such as folders and files managed by the CMS system, and are different from the ones that we saw for the portal assets earlier in this chapter.

The following features are supported by the security system of the portal CMS:

- The permissions, 'Read', 'Write', and 'Manage' can be assigned at the CMS node level (Both Files and Folders are treated as CMS nodes)

- The Permissions are propagated recursively down a folder hierarchy

- Any Permissions specified explicitly on the CMS Node overrides the policy inherited via recursive propagation

- Permissions can be managed by using the CMS Admin GUI tool via the 'Secure Node' feature

The portal CMS permission matrix can be seen in the following table:

Permissions	Allowed Actions	Implies
Read	Read contents of a Folder, a File, and its versions	N/A
Write	Create and Update new Folders and Files	Read Access
Manage	Delete/Copy/Move/Rename Folders and Files	Read and Write Access

CMS content can be secured via the JBoss portal server admin console, by logging in as **admin** and clicking on the **CMS** tab. After selecting the appropriate node, we need to select the option called **secure** in the **Select Action** pull-down, to ensure the security of the contents. In our example, we will look at the security configuration options for the default page.

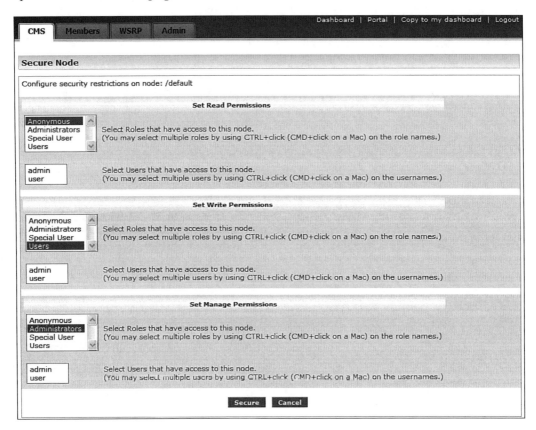

We can now assign various security constraints to specific users.

CMS security configuration

Apart from the admin console, the configuration for CMS Security can be specified in the jboss-portal.sar/portal-cms.sar/META-INF/jboss-service.xml file.

CMS super user

A CMS super user, like a UNIX super user, has a designated role given by the portal server, and comes with the rights to edit, accept, and delete assets. Care should be taken while using this role due to the risks associated with the role.

```
15.2.1.2. CMS Security Console
```

CMS security console

The CMS security console is used to assign correct permissions to all of the nodes and content in the CMS. Only portal users belonging to a specified role can access the console. Typically, this is the *Admin* role for the server.

Summary

In this chapter, we have discussed the various aspects of security as they relate to the JBoss portal server and its functional components—the portal objects. JBoss portal allows a fine-grained level of control of the portal objects, such as portal instances, pages, and portlets. The security constraints are complemented by a robust set of options for performing authentication and authorization. Similar to portal object configuration, JBoss portal also offers options to secure assets.

Security is an important function of an application, and JBoss portal offers a varied set of options that allow the building of highly-secure enterprise applications on the portal server.

In the next chapter, we will go out of the domain of our applications and discuss ways to integrate with other applications in the enterprise and in the outside world.

10

Web Services and Portlets

Up to now, we have been talking largely about creating functions and features within the portal server. With wider acceptance of SOAP-based services today, leveraging portlet functionality on remote servers can be of immense value. **Web Services for Remote Portlets (WSRP)** is a specification that allows portal applications to incorporate portlets that are hosted on remote servers, including presentation markup using SOAP-based web services.

Service Oriented Architecture (SOA) is built upon the concept of providing business functions through loosely-coupled, re-usable services. WSRP facilitates such integration by providing interfaces for re-using existing presentation-oriented portlets. Because their inclusion involves almost no additional development effort and only minor configuration changes, remote portlets are of significant value in an enterprise.

In this chapter, we will discuss the basics of remoting portlets, before going into a few implementations using some real-world examples.

Remoting in portal servers

The integration of remote services with clearly-defined interfaces, into a loosely-coupled architecture, has been the cornerstone of application development for a while now. The desire to share existing functionality and investment while cleanly separating business functions has been prevalent since before the advent of today's accepted norms such as SOA. However, the use of web services and SOAP-based communication has significantly increased the efficiency of applications leveraging remote functionality. Web services offer a simple and technology-agnostic option for integrating remote functions with a local application.

Portals are, by and large, a collection of business applications, and have direct relevance to the end users. A typical enterprise might end up with a few portal servers and quite some redundancies in the functionality on each of them. Hence, it seems almost intuitive that enterprises, tuned to the concept of services, would want a way of sharing existing functionality. There are many approaches to making remote calls and executing remote functionality using traditional methods such as RMI, IIOP, or even plain HTTP POSTS/GETs. However, the portal platform's standardization on web services for remoting offers some unique advantages in terms of portability, simplicity, and implementation.

The WSRP was born out of such a need. It offers a mechanism for portlets to be re-used and consumed by others, and also provides a container for remote portlets from different sources to be accessed and aggregated through a single portal.

Web Service for Remote Portlets

The Web Service for Remote Portlets specification, created by the joint efforts of the **Web Services for Interactive Applications (WSIA)** and **WSRP OASIS Technical** committees, defines the interface for accessing and creating presentation-oriented web services.

Traditional web services are data-oriented, and require consumer applications to create their own user interface and interact with their unique interface. Although quite useful, they can still be quite cumbersome to create and manage, when the need is for easy and dynamic aggregation of business functions. WSRP seeks to alleviate both of these issues by providing a specification for presentation-oriented web services that integrate both at the application and presentation levels, thus exposing a remote business function in its entirety, along with its user interface.

The official web site of WSRP, at `http://www.oasis-open.org/committees/wsrp/`, offers detailed information about the specification, including a good primer that provides a technical overview of the concepts. It is strongly recommended that every portlet developer reads this.

We can summarize the drivers for using WSRP in portal applications, by considering the following two scenarios, when they are best applicable:

1. As a provider of shareable portlets, a portal server can create specific portlets that have cross-enterprise applicability and host them on a single server for multiple consumers across the enterprise. A good example is a service locator mapping function. A single area in the company with cartographic and mapping knowledge can develop the portlet and expose it as a WSRP producer. Any other unit of the company can access this functionality without having to build such a portlet themselves.

2. As a consumer, instead of creating portlet functionality from scratch, a portal server can re-use an existing investment by aggregating presentation-oriented portlets using WSRP. A good example is a corporate Intranet portal. A corporate Intranet portal is, in most cases, an aggregated view of all of the functions that employees care for and use. Every department can now host its functionalities, such as time reporting, expense management, and so on, as WSRP portlets, which the corporate portal can consume, and aggregate the user interface.

The specification is based on the requirements and proposals provided to the technical committees. It is platform-independent and is built on existing web and web services standards such as SSL, URL, WSDL, SOAP, and so on.

Let us review the salient concepts and components that facilitate WSRP implementation in portal servers.

WSRP actors

To better understand the concepts and the operation of a typical WSRP-enabled application, let us first look at the various components or actors that are playing significant roles in the whole flow.

The basic idea of the specification is that, on request from an end user, a Consumer communicates with a Producer, which in turn provides the interface, including the user experience, to the customer. A Producer is a remote portlet that hosts presentation-oriented web services, and that accept requests and renders page fragment markup back to the Consumer of the service.

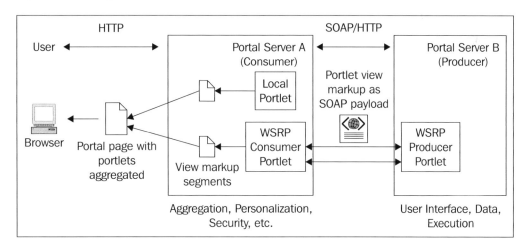

Portlet

A WSRP portlet here adds to the traditional definition, of a portlet by being hosted as a producer web service and generating markup along with processing requests. The functionality and the logic are housed in the portlet and conform to the Producer environment, to provide support for remote web service calls.

Producer

Producers host portlets remotely, as shown in the preceding figure by Portal Server B, and are responsible for providing a set of web service interfaces prescribed by WSRP. These interfaces are:

- **Service Description**: This is a required interface that indicates the functions and capabilities provided by a remote producer through its portlets. It includes a definition of and meta information for the portlet, and allows remote Consumers to inquire and determine the properties required for effective connection to the Producer. The self-description interface, in a way, acts as a definition of the service, and typically includes information such as registration or cookie requirements before a Consumer can connect to the Producer.

- **Markup**: This is another required interface used by Consumers to interact with Producers that provide markup fragments. When a Consumer forwards a request on behalf of the end user to the Producer, it uses this interface to obtain the markup information from the Producer.

- **Portlet Management**: This is an optional interface that provides access to the portlet life cycle of the Producer, allowing a Consumer to manage the behavior of the portlet and its state.

  A Portlet is identified with a `portletHandle`, and Consumers use this handle to communicate with the portlet. A portlet exposed by the Producer is pre-configured and cannot be modified by default. Such portlets are called **Producer Managed Portlets**. However, if the Producer offers the Property Management Interface, the life cycle of the Portlet can be managed by the Consumer. Such portlets are called **Consumer Managed Portlets**. A Consumer can even use this interface to clone Portlets and customize their behavior.

- **Registration**: This is an optional interface that is primarily used to indicate to the Consumer that the Producer requires registration in order to be able to use the service. The Consumer can have access to the service description and markup interface only after the registration conditions prescribed by the interface have been satisfied.

The following WSDL listing of a Producer service demonstrates all of the preceding interfaces:

```
<wsdl:definitions targetNamespace="urn:oasis:names:tc:wsrp:v1:wsdl">
    <import namespace="urn:oasis:names:tc:wsrp:v1:bind"
            location="http://www.oasis-open.org/committees/wsrp/
                      specifications/version1/wsrp_v1_bindings.wsdl" />
    <wsdl:service name="WSRPService">
        <wsdl:port binding="bind:WSRP_v1_Markup_Binding_SOAP"
            name="WSRPBaseService">
            <soap:addresslocation="http://portalstandards.oracle.com:80
                              /portletapp/portlets/WSRPBaseService" />
        </wsdl:port>
        <wsdl:port
            binding="bind:WSRP_v1_ServiceDescription_Binding_SOAP"
            name="WSRPServiceDescriptionService">
            <soap:addresslocation="http://portalstandards.oracle.com:80
                    /portletapp/portlets/WSRPServiceDescriptionService" />
        </wsdl:port>
        <wsdl:port binding="bind:WSRP_v1_Registration_Binding_SOAP"
            name="WSRPRegistrationService">
            <soap:addresslocation="http://portalstandards.oracle.com:80
                          /portletapp/portlets/WSRPRegistrationService" />
        </wsdl:port>
        <wsdl:port
            binding="bind:WSRP_v1_PortletManagement_Binding_SOAP"
            name="WSRPPortletManagementService">
            <soap:addresslocation="http://portalstandards.oracle.com:80
                    /portletapp/portlets/WSRPPortletManagementService" />
        </wsdl:port>
    </wsdl:service>
</wsdl:definitions>
```

Consumer

A Consumer in a WSRP is an intermediary, as shown in the previous figure by Portal Server A. The Consumer makes requests to the Producer on behalf of the end user using the portal application from a browser. Consumers interact with the presentation-oriented web services offered by Producers and aggregate the markup responses provided by the Producers. Consumers using WSRP are usually other portals, but can also include standard enterprise applications that make the call to the Producers and use the markup returned to create an aggregated view. Because the Consumer acts as a routing switch between an end user and a Producer, the end user trusts the Consumer on all of the security and privacy issues.

End user

The end user is the user of the system who is invoking the portal application on the browser, and for whom the Consumer aggregates the markup information received from the remote Producers. The markup fragments aggregated by the Consumer are independent of the end user interface, but functions such as client-side scripting, DHTML processing, validation and so on, are usually passed on to the end-user interface for efficiency and performance-related reasons.

Process flow

Now that we understand the various actors in a typical WSRP interaction, it might be helpful if we went through the process flow step-by-step to better reinforce the idea.

Before an end-user makes a request, a Consumer creates a reference to the Producer and makes the interface available to the end user. The following flow is typical, but some of the events listed in it are optional.

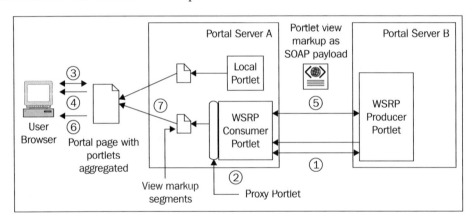

1. When the portal is initialized during startup, the Consumer invokes the URL of the web service end-point of the Producer. It then gets a description of the service capabilities, along with the Producer's meta information and registration requirements, if any.

   With the appropriate requirements satisfied, the Consumer establishes a relationship with the Producer. The Consumer and Producer exchange information, including those related to capabilities, registration, and security.

2. The Consumer then creates a proxy portlet to represent the Producer.

3. When the end user on the browser invokes the portal application, the Consumer retrieves the information related to the user's security credentials, and so on, in addition to providing the end user with aggregated markup including portlets and portal pages.

4. The end user, using a browser, requests a page by invoking the Consumer URL. Alternatively, instead of a human user, these requests can also be triggered by automatic page refreshes.

5. The Consumer determines the appropriate Producer portlet and the nature of the invocation requested, and then invokes the Producer, which in turn returns the portlet markup and a portlet state.

6. The Consumer then aggregates the markup into a page and sends this back to the browser.

7. Once the Producer has satisfied the requests of the Consumer, both of the actors have the option to end their relationship. If so decided upon, the relationship is terminated and the related resources are cleaned up.

WSRP Use Profiles

The WSRP Use Profile provides general guidelines, at a high-level, for implementing the functionality of a Producer or a Consumer. Portals are free to choose from the options provided to create the best solution stack.

The idea is to provide a broad spectrum of options spread across various categories, so that portal implementations can clearly articulate support for advanced features in some areas, but simple features in some others.

Use Profile levels indicate the categories of features that are required to be provided. The Producer profile has three levels, each with increasing complexity and richness of features. Let's look at each of these levels in detail.

Producer levels

The Use Profile for a Producer includes three levels, 'Base', 'Simple' and "Complex. Let us look at them in detail

Base

- Implements only the MUST interfaces
- No state (session or persistent) — uses opaque mechanism to send state back to Consumer
- No cloning
- No initialization required
- Does not rewrite URLs in markup
- Does not require registration

Simple

- May request initialization—could store state in cookies
- Supports cloning
- May require registration (out-of-band)
- Session state; creates and sends session handles to the Consumer

Complex

- May rewrite URLs (requires Consumer templates)
- May offer both in-band and out-of-band registration
- Persistent local state
- May support grouping of portlets

Consumer levels

However, there are four levels in the Use Profile for a Consumer. It adds a 'Medium' level to 'Base', 'Simple', and 'Complex', to address some intermediate requirements. Let's look at these in detail.

Base

- Implements only the MUST interfaces
- VIEW mode, NORMAL window state only
- Supplies no user information (portlet may fault or degrade functionality in response)
- Rewrites URLs
- Initializes the Producer if required (`initCookie`)
- Handles Producer cookies
- Limited markup types (for example, HTML)
- Does not clone (`readOnly`—may limit functionality of portlets that offer personalization)
- No in-band registration

Simple

- Support for standard modes and window states
- Support for in-band registration
- Supplies basic user information (for example, identity and authorization type)
- Handles implicit clones (`cloneBeforeWrite`)

Medium

- Complex user management; willingness to supply standard/extended user attributes
- Multiple markup types (for example, HTML and WML)
- Caching according to Producer-supplied cache control.
- May explicitly clone portlets
- May supply URL rewrite templates to a Producer that is capable of rewriting URLs in portlet markup

Complex

- May support custom window states and/or modes
- Multiple levels of user access (user categories)
- Localization
- May use explicit property-setting mechanism — create custom UI for property management

WSRP in JBoss portal

JBoss portal provides support for WSRP and helps the development of presentation-oriented portlets that can either be consumed by external aggregation engines, or can help presentation-oriented remote portlets of Consumers. However, JBoss portal server's support for WSRP is constrained to some extent by the scenarios defined in the WSRP Use Profiles document. We saw a brief overview of these in the previous section of this chapter.

As a WSRP Producer, JBoss provides a *Simple* level of support, except for "out-of-band registration". Instead, it supports "in-band registration" and a persistent local state — a feature in the *Complex* state.

As a Consumer, JBoss provides *Medium* level support for WSRP, with the exception of markup being limited to HTML only. This is primarily because, as a portal, HTML markup is the only markup possible. However, portlet cloning and Portlet Management interfaces are supported.

Caching is supported for the Producer and the Consumer at Level 1. Although cookie handling is supported in Consumers, the initialization of cookies is supported in Producers. CSS is also supported in both Consumers and Producers. The server, however, doesn't support custom windows states or modes.

WSRP implementation support

WSRP support in JBoss portal is provided by the **portal-wsrp.sar** service archive, which is provided as part of the `jboss-portal.sar` service archive. JBoss portal provides full support for WSRP 1.0 interfaces, and offers support for Consumer and Provider services within the bounds of the Use Profile. Hence, for a new install, WSRP is automatically enabled on the platform.

The following figure shows the location of the service archive in relation to the main **jboss-portal** service archive:

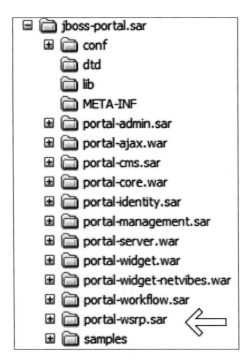

Enabling remoting in portlets

A JBoss portlet can be made remotable by configuring the appropriate parameters in the configuration files. By default, JBoss portal server doesn't make its portlets available for remote Consumers. Hence, every portlet that needs to be exposed as a remote service, needs to be individually enabled in the portlet configuration file `jboss-portlet.xml`.

The `jboss-portlet.xml` file, needs an entry for the portlet with a `<remotable>` tag set to `true`.

If this file doesn't exist, then a new file needs to be created.

The following code shows how a sample portlet, "SayHello", has been enabled for remoting:

```
<?xml version="1.0" standalone="yes"?>
<!DOCTYPE portlet-app PUBLIC "-//JBoss Portal//DTD JBoss Portlet
  2.7//EN"
         "http://www.jboss.org/portal/dtd/jboss-portlet_2_7.dtd">
<portlet-app>
   <portlet>
      <portlet-name>SayHelloPortlet</portlet-name>
      <remotable>true</remotable>
   </portlet>
</portlet-app>
```

To enable multiple portlets in an application, the `<remotable>true</remotable>` element needs to be moved to the root `portlet-app` node, as shown in the following code:

```
<?xml version="1.0" standalone="yes"?>
<!DOCTYPE portlet-app PUBLIC "-//JBoss Portal//DTD JBoss Portlet
  2.7//EN"
         "http://www.jboss.org/portal/dtd/jboss-portlet_2_7.dtd">
<portlet-app>
<remotable>true</remotable>
   <portlet>
      <portlet-name>SayHelloRemotePortlet</portlet-name>
   </portlet>
   <portlet>
      <portlet-name>SayHelloLocalPortlet</portlet-name>
      <remotable>false</remotable>
   </portlet>
</portlet-app>
```

Moving the element to the root node enables all the portlets for remoting. However, as seen in the preceding example, by explicitly adding the `<remotable>false</remotable>` element, we have excluded this particular portlet from being enabled for remoting.

Configuring WSRP producer

The JBoss portal's Producer is automatically set up when you deploy a portal instance with the WSRP service.

The WSDL for the portal Producer can be accessed at `http://{hostname}:{port}/portal-wsrp/MarkupService?wsdl`.

The end point URLs are accessible at:

- `http://{hostname}:{port}/portal-wsrp/ServiceDescriptionService`
- `http://{hostname}:{port}/portal-wsrp/MarkupService`
- `http://{hostname}:{port}/portal-wsrp/RegistrationService`
- `http://{hostname}:{port}/portal-wsrp/PortletManagementService`

The default hostname is `localhost`, and the default port is `8080`.

In the following sections, we will talk about how a Producer can be configured to provide granular access control.

Producer configuration

The Producer can be configured on the JBoss portal platform either by using the WSRP administrative interface, or by editing the `conf/config.xml` file, which can be found in the `portal-wsrp.sar` service archive.

Typical elements that can be configured are access control and registration requirements. An XML Schema for the configuration format is available at `jboss-portal.sar/portal-wsrp.sar/xsd/jboss-wsrp-producer_2_7.xsd`, and a (legacy) DTD is available at `jboss-portal.sar/portal-wsrp.sar/dtd/jboss-wsrp-producer_2_6.dtd`.

The default Producer configuration requires Consumers requesting for the services to register, but doesn't require any registration properties. Hence, unless the Consumer is registered, the list of services won't be available. The Producer uses the default `org.jboss.portal.registration.policies.DefaultRegistrationPolicy` and `org.jboss.portal.registration.policies.DefaultRegistrationPropertyValidator` to determine if the provided registration information is valid.

The **Producer Configuration** tab can be found on the **WSRP** tabbed page of the **Admin** portal. The following screenshot illustrates the default screen and the various configuration options:

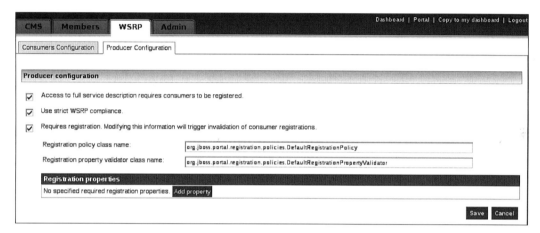

Customization

Various elements can now be configured, including any new additional registration properties that a Consumer would have to provide in order to successfully access the portlets provided.

Optionally, if we want to allow unregistered Consumers to access our portlets and list them, but do not want to allow interaction with them without registration, then we can deselect the first checkbox titled **Access to full service description requires consumers to be registered**, and select the checkbox titled **Requires registration. Modifying this information will trigger the invalidation of consumer registrations**.

Similarly, if we want to require that Consumers enter a registration property, we can create a property by clicking on the **Add property** button. We add a new property called **username** and provide a label to it. On saving, we now have the constraints defined for our Producer, including the registration requirements to access portlets, along with the required registration property.

Just like other elements on the configuration screen, the registration policy classes can also be customized by providing an implementation of the `RegistrationPolicy` and `RegistrationPropertyValidator` classes. This allows customized control over the policies that govern the Producer's behavior when it is exposed to remote Consumers.

Configuring WSRP consumer

The Consumers can be created and configured in a number of ways. It all depends on whether we are providing the URL for the WSDL or the URL for the end points. JBoss portal provides both of these options.

The first step in consuming the remote WSRP portlet is to configure the remote portlet in the **Consumer Configuration** option of the **Admin** account. To configure remote portlet, we can either use the provided Admin portlet or add entries to WSRP producer descriptor. Let's first look at using the admin portlet.

Remote producer configuration using Admin portlet

To consume a remote portlet, we first need to register the WSRP Producer that is providing the service. In our example, we will configure Oracle's public WSRP service.

The configuration portlet for configuring Consumers can be found in the portal's **Admin** section under the admin account, on the **WSRP** tabbed page. As shown in the following screenshot, we will enter a new Consumer name called **Oracle**, and click on **Create Consumer**.

A Consumer portlet can either be **active** or **inactive**. When a Consumer portlet is **active**, it is listed in the portlet listing, and if it is **inactive** it will be taken off the provider list. Sometimes, the remote Producer information can become stale. Hence, a refresh is needed to update any expired interfaces and incompletely-fetched service descriptions.

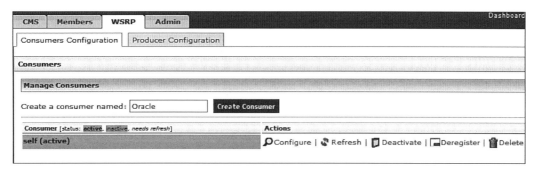

We are then taken to the next screen, where we need to enter the cache expiration time and the endpoint URL.

As shown in the following screenshot, we enter the following information:

Cache expiration: 300 (seconds before expiration)

Endpoint configuration: http://portalstandards.oracle.com/portletapp/portlets?WSDL

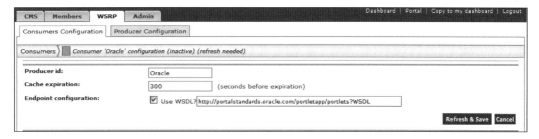

When the form is saved, the container will invoke the end point and provide an appropriate message back to the console. In our case, the container didn't find any problems invoking and parsing the endpoint, which results in a message, as shown in the following screenshot. This also indicates that the service doesn't have any need for registration specification. Otherwise, we will see an error message with a request to complete the registration information. The registration information for a Producer is specific to that producer, and sometimes it is necessary to check the Producer documentation to get the correct information.

The Consumer for the **Oracle** Producer is now configured, and the portlets offered by the remote Producer should be available for use.

Using the WSDL is the most convenient and efficient option. However, in scenarios where WSDL is not available, the Producer can be configured using the provided interfaces. Just deselect the **Use WSDL?** checkbox, and you should see input fields for various service interfaces.

The following screenshot shows how the Producer is configured using the interface URLs:

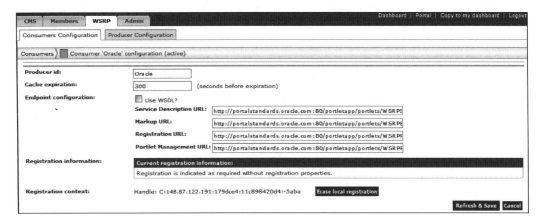

Remote producer configuration using the WSRP producer descriptor

If, for some reason, we don't want to use the provided portlet to configure the Consumer, we can achieve the same results by creating a descriptor file and adding the relevant entries to it.

We create a descriptor file called `provider-oracle-wsrp.xml`. The name is irrelevant, as long as it ends in `-wsrp.xml`.

A DTD and an XML Schema for WSRP Producer XML descriptors are available in `jboss-portal.sar/portal-wsrp.sar/dtd/jboss-wsrp-consumer_2_7.dtd` and `jboss-portal.sar/portal-wsrp.sar/xsd/jboss-wsrp-consumer_2_7.xsd`.

The descriptor file for our Oracle Producer will look like this:

```
<?xml version='1.0' encoding='UTF-8' ?>
<!DOCTYPE deployments PUBLIC "-//JBoss Portal//DTD WSRP Remote
  Producer Configuration 2.7//EN"
   "http://www.jboss.org/portal/dtd/jboss-wsrp-consumer_2_7.dtd">
<deployments>
  <deployment>
    <wsrp-producer id="Oracle" expiration-cache="300">
      <endpoint-wsdl-url>
          http://portalstandards.oracle.com/portletapp/portlets?WSDL
      </endpoint-wsdl-url>
    </wsrp-producer>
  </deployment>
</deployments>
```

Any registration requirements would have been sub-elements under `<wsrp-producer>`.

The file is then placed in the JBoss portal deploy directory. When deployed, the server will pick up the file, establish a connection to the Provider, and make the portlet available.

We can now go back to the **Portlet Definitions** tab on the **Admin** section to see all of the portlets available on the portal. If we filter the list by selecting **Oracle** in the drop-down, we will see all of the portlets that are provided remotely by Oracle are enabled, due to our portlet configuration.

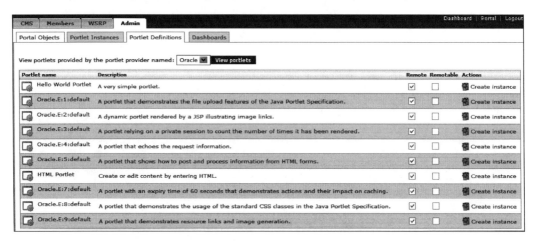

Managing consumer configuration

As discussed earlier, sometimes a remote portlet requests additional registration information to be considered for enabling remote services. Apart from the basic security functions, this registration information helps to provide access control to various public portlets, based on the registration level.

The following screenshot shows the registration failure for a third-party service called **BEA** service, which is looking for a value for the field `consumerRole`. Coincidentally, here, the options are provided, but this is not always the case. In most cases, we are required to contact the service provider, or refer to their documentation.

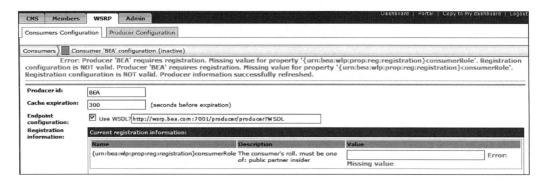

Once an acceptable value has been entered, the portal server successfully registers the Producer and makes the portlets available for that level, as seen in the following screenshot:

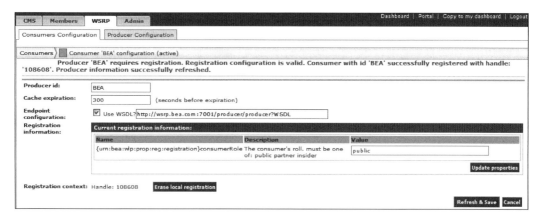

Instantiation of a remote portlet

Once the portlets are configured, as we saw earlier, they are visible on the **Portlet Definitions** tabbed page of the **Admin** console. We can instantiate the portlet by using the link next to it. This will add an entry for the portlet on the **Portlet Instances** tab, along with the current instances.

An instantiated portlet can be included in any portal page layout, just like any local portlet. Although the portlet instances look and behave like a local portlet, WSRP allows it to communicate transparently and execute its functions on the remote server, while serving the needs of the local portal application.

Summary

Web services have proven to bring significant value to enterprises. The popularity of SOA in large enterprises drives the need for platforms that allow easy integration and re-use of existing investments to create loosely-coupled business functions. The WSRP specification goes a long way to helping build such business services that can be easily integrated with almost no development effort, in order to provide immediate business value.

We have seen the ease with which portlets can be exposed as remotely-available services, and how remote services can be consumed relatively effortlessly. The biggest value of WSRP is that it takes the principle of service integration a step further by integrating not only at a functional business level but also at the user interface level, thereby providing a services architecture that requires no additional development. The specification is still evolving, and we can look forward to portals playing a much bigger role in building enterprise re-usable services, in the future.

11
Portlet Coordination and Filters

Portal and portlet-driven applications have become popular largely due to the rich features they offer, combined with the limited effort required to build them. With the newer portal specification, JSR-286, it is now possible to implement advanced features that were previously either not possible, or required complex workarounds. With these features now built into the specification, the JBoss portal server can offer them by default, and in a standard manner. However, no specification is comprehensive, and to address scenarios not covered by the specification, JBoss portal provides a set of proprietary implementations that fill the gap.

In this chapter, we will discuss some of the features included in the new portlet specification, such as portlet co-ordination and filters. With the advent of a loosely-coupled architecture and functionality sharing, the value of inter-portlet communication and coordination has gained wider preference in the industry. Similarly, filters provide functionality that addresses a much needed gap for finer control in the execution of a portlet.

Going from JSR-168 to JSR-286

Java Specification Request (JSR) 168 was released in 2003, and since then, there have been numerous implementations platforms, and portal applications on these platforms. Just as with any other technology, with the increasing use and exploitation of features, the limits and shortcomings of the specifications began to surface. Inter-portlet communication or co-ordination between portlets has gained a lot of significance in recent times. JSR-168 does address inter-portlet communication to a certain limited extent, but left the implementation to portal providers. This has, hence, resulted in custom proprietary portlet solutions, which makes the portlets non-portable as a whole. To fill this gap, and to cover some other evolving concepts such as an enhanced version of WSRP, the industry as a whole felt the need for an update to the specification. Thus, JSR-286, or Java Portlet Specification version 2.0, was born. The final version of the specification was approved and released in 2008. WSRP 2.0, the newer standard for remote portlet communication, was created by the OASIS standards body, and they are evolving the standard in tandem with portal specification JSR-286, to ensure compatibility and consistency from day one. JBoss portal 2.7.0 is the first general-availability release of a portal server supporting JSR-286. It also provides a standalone portlet container that can be implemented without requiring you to install JBoss portal server.

Some of the features introduced in the first draft of JSR 286 are as follows:

- **Events**: These enable inter-portlet communication through event transfer between portlets
- **Shared render parameters**: These provide options for portlets to control parameter sharing with other portlets
- **Resource serving**: These allow portlets to serve resources within the portlet context
- **Portlet Filters**: These allow the dynamic transformation of the content of portlet requests and responses

Other JSR-286 features include alignment with J2SE 5.0, better AJAX support, and better support for web frameworks (Spring, Struts, and so on).

In the next few sections, we will dive deeper into events, shared render parameters, and portlet filters.

Portlet coordination and inter-portlet communication

Inter-portlet communication is an interesting and useful concept. Although independent portlet functionality has its own value, allowing portlets to communicate with each others can offer a richer, more composite functionality. Secondly, enterprises create portal applications for multiple functions and sometimes deploy third-party portal applications. Inter-portlet communication allows for the seamless integration of the features and functionality of these disparate portlets, to provide a cohesive and complementary set of functions.

Due to the lack of clarity on IPC in JSR-168, there was no standard way of implementing inter-portlet communication. The specification didn't address the capability of sending events between portlets. Events could be sent only within a single portlet application, and not across portlet applications, due to the session scope being limited to the portlet's applications session scope. This is especially a problem because enterprises have complex portal implementations with portlets spread across multiple applications, which cannot be grouped under the same portal application in order to allow them to communicate. Every vendor addressed these issues with its own proprietary solutions, resulting with implementations that were heavily dependant on the platform and inconsistent, defeating the purpose of the portlet standard specification.

However, the new Portlet 2.0 specification standardized inter-portlet communication, or portlet coordination as it is called, resulting in out-of-the-box support for features and configurations that help portlets to communicate with each other. The coordination features are based on a loosely-coupled, publish—subscribe model, and the participating portlets are not required to have advance knowledge of each other's design, usage, and behavior. As the connections between the portlets are actually established during runtime, at the time of development, the portlets need to just define the data elements used during inter-portlet communication. This allows the end user to create a whole new composite set of applications using portlets, using portlets not only from within the same application, but also from other applications, resulting, in some cases, in a Web 2.0 style mashup behavior.

JSR-286 added the following capabilities to facilitate portlet co-ordination:

- Portlet events that a portlet can receive and send
- Public render parameters that share render state across portlets

Before we go full steam ahead with an example, let's understand how the specification defines events-based and public render parameter-based coordination.

Portlet events

Portlet events are actions that are generated by portlets to indicate a certain change of state, and are not something that are directly triggered by a user action. These events can also be the consequence of a direct user action on a different portlet. A portlet can both generate events and receive them. The events are not guaranteed for delivery, and are not a substitute for reliable messaging options.

The basic flow of an event appears as follows:

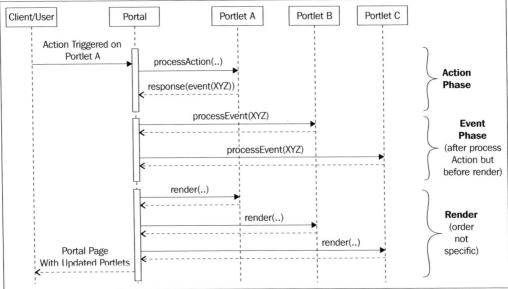

A **publishing portlet** is one that sets event and informs the portal about it. A **processing portlet** is one that listens for an event and then processes it. As described in the sequence diagram, the portlet that sets the events is Portlet A. Here, the event publishing portlet is triggered by user activity on the portlet. The portlet sets the events in its action phase. After the action phase and before the render phase, JSR-286 creates a new "event" phase in the portlet life cycle with a life cycle method, processEvent. All of the portlets, here Portlet B and Portlet C, that want to receive the event, and the event processing portlets, need to implement the processEvent method that will be invoked by the container in the event phase. Once the subscriber portlets B and C finish executing the processEvent methods, the container starts the rendering phase for each of the portlets on the page, resulting in the final page with updated portlets, based on an action on a single portlet.

However, the specification doesn't define how the portlets are wired together, or their relation to the portal page. It is left to the portal server providers to implement these aspects in their own way.

To understand this better, in the coming sections, we will create event-based coordination using our example application.

Public render parameters

We have talked briefly about public render parameters as they relate to implementing asynchronous request response in our chapter on AJAX. However, these parameters serve a broader purpose of establishing communication between portlets.

Public render parameters can be shared across portlets and portal pages. They are not restricted to the portlet application, and span multiple applications. It is a lightweight coordination model based on HTTP GET, and provides a very simple approach for passing parameters between portlets.

The shared parameters are defined in `portlet.xml` and declared as being public.

Consider the following scenario in which there are two portlets in an application called Portlet A and Portlet B. Portlet A accepts the account number as a parameter for retrieving customer information. Portlet B is a second portlet that uses the same account number to provide information related to the product that the user owns. This is a typical up-sell/cross-sell marketing technique.

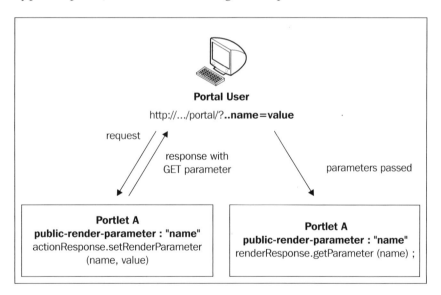

Now, suppose that the same parameter is shared between the two portlets as a shared render parameter named "name". When the user enters the account number for retrieving account information in Portlet A, Portlet B will also be able to access the account ID value because it also receives the parameter, "name". This will allow Portlet B to also provide customized products that best fit the needs of the user, without interfering with the user's basic experience on the web site.

Hence, we can see that defining public render parameters provides an easy and efficient way of executing inter-portlet coordination. This differs from events in many ways, the most important being the fact that portlets using shared render parameters do not get notified when things change, as is the case with events. However, they are quite useful in several scenarios where we have simple needs.

In the next section, we will see, using an example, how we can implement portlet coordination using public render parameters.

Portlet coordination in JBoss portal

Although coordination has become a standard recently, JBoss portal has always offered an inter-portlet communication feature. Hence, with the implementation of the new specification, there are two ways to achieve inter-portlet communication in JBoss portal:

- Using the traditional JSR-168: JBoss portal server has always provided a mechanism for inter-portlet communication using events and its own proprietary implementation using listeners
- Using JSR-286 style portlet coordination: JBoss portal server fully supports JSR-286 and offers a strong set of features for portlet coordination that can be wired at runtime. This approach includes both of the options provided by the specification:
    - Events-based
    - Shared render parameters-based

    JBoss portal provides some custom enhancements to JSR-286 coordination which makes it much more useful and flexible. We will discuss these features after we discuss the standard coordination capabilities.

In this section, we will put all of our concepts to practice and try to fully understand coordination by using examples on the JBoss portal server platform.

We will use the "MyCompany" portal application that we have been using throughout this book to demonstrate portlet coordination and JBoss portal server inter-portlet communication.

JSR-168 inter-portlet communication

Whereas Portlet 2.0 offers a standardized way of implementing portlet coordination, for JSR-168-based implementations, JBoss portal server has always offered an option to facilitate inter-portlet communication using its own proprietary implementation.

This is still a viable option, especially if we are on the JBoss portal platform. It is important to note, however, that such an implementation is not portable and doesn't have all of the capabilities of the coordination model. Also, with portlet coordination now a standard part of the specification, the future of such an implementation is uncertain.

The JBoss implementation is built on listeners that react to the events and execute functionality. There are three steps involved in developing inter-portlet communication:

1. Edit portlets and create listener methods
2. Configure listeners and portlets
3. Package and deploy

Let's walk through these steps with an example. For consistency and easy comparison, we will continue to use our example of DbPortlet interacting with AssetPortlet, with the variable empId.

Coding listener and portlets

Given that we are going to deal with custom events, we need to declare a listener to receive these events. A Listener class is created as an inner class of the Portlet class.

In our caller-recipient example, with DbPortlet being the caller and AssetPortlet being the recipient, the listener is declared in AssetPortlet, which DbPortlet will be invoking.

```
public static class Listener implements PortalNodeEventListener
{
    public PortalNodeEvent onEvent(PortalNodeEventContext
            context, PortalNodeEvent event)
    {
        PortalNode node = event.getNode();

        // Get node name
        String nodeName = node.getName();

        // See if we need to create a new event or not
        WindowActionEvent newEvent = null;
        if (nodeName.equals("DbPortletWindow") && event
            instanceof WindowActionEvent)
        {
            // Find dest window
            WindowActionEvent wae = (WindowActionEvent)event;
            PortalNode destWindow =  node.resolve
```

```
                                        ("../AssetPortletWindow");
            if (destWindow != null)
            {
                // We can redirect
                newEvent = new WindowActionEvent(destWindow);
                newEvent.setParameters(wae.getParameters());
            }
        }
        //
        if (newEvent != null)
        {
            // If we have a new event return it
            return newEvent;
        }
        else
        {
            return context.dispatch();
        }
    }
}
```

Here, we should note some of the important items in this listener class. Logic is used to determine if the requesting node was DbPortlet:

```
(nodeName.equals("DbPortletWindow")
```

We get the current window object so that we can dispatch the event to it:

```
PortalNode destWindow = node.resolve("../AssetPortletWindow");
```

We wet the original parameters from DbPortlet so that AssetPortlet can access them in its processAction():

```
newEvent.setParameters(wae.getParameters());
```

Once we have the listener inner class created, we can retrieve parameters from our special JBossActionRequest class.

```
    public void processAction(JBossActionRequest request,
        JBossActionResponse response)
        throws PortletException, PortletSecurityException,
        IOException {
        String empId = request.getParameter("empId");

        actionResponse.setRenderParameters(request.getParameterMap());

    }
```

Setting the render parameters will pass the values to the AssetPortlet's, `doView()` method.

Configuring the listener and portlets

To ensure that the listener is loaded and executed, we need to add entries both in the service descriptor and in the portlet deployment descriptors.

Service descriptor

Listeners intercept requests and responses, and are required for effective IPC. The listener is declared as an `mbean` in the service descriptor, as shown in the following example under `mycompany.sar/META-INF/jboss-service.xml`:

```
<server>
    <!-- Portlet 1.0 listener-based IPC -->
    <mbean
        code="org.jboss.portal.core.event.
              PortalEventListenerServiceImpl"
        name="portal:service=ListenerService,type=empId_listener"
        xmbean-dd=""
        xmbean-code="org.jboss.portal.jems.as.system.
                     JBossServiceModelMBean">
        <xmbean/>
        <depends
            optional-attribute-name="Registry"
            proxy-type="attribute">portal:service=ListenerRegistry
        </depends>
        <attribute name="RegistryId">empId_listener</attribute>
        <attribute name="ListenerClassName">
            org.mycompany.portlet.asset.AssetPortlet$Listener
        </attribute>
    </mbean>
</server>
```

There is no need to change the values in the configuration file except in the following cases:

- `name`: Both the `mbean` type and the `RegistryId` values must match
- `ListenerClassName`: This is the full path to the listening portet's inner class that acts as the listener

The service descriptor is packaged as a service archive file named `mycompany.sar`.

Portal descriptor

The reference to the listener is also added to the `mycompany-object.xml` at the page level, so the portal recognizes it when the page is invoked.

```
<deployment>
    <if-exists>overwrite</if-exists>
    <parent-ref/>
    <portal>
      <portal-name>mycompany</portal-name>
      <parent-ref>default</parent-ref>
      <if-exists>overwrite</if-exists>
      <page>
          <page-name>default</page-name>
          <listener> empId_listener</listener>
          <properties/>
          ...
      </page>
    </portal>
</deployment>
```

It is important to note that the `listener` value has the same `name` value as in the service descriptor.

Deploying portlets

We deploy the portal application along with the service descriptor. The service descriptor initializes the listener and from there on, the behavior is very similar to we have seen when using JSR-286 event-based and public render parameter-based implementations.

The `AssetPortlet`, as in other cases, can operate independently as well as in coordination with the `DbPortlet`.

Portlet events-based coordination

Implementing portlet coordination is substantially different and easier in the new Portlet 2.0 specification. Let's look at how the new events-based coordination works. As we can see in the following figure, events are triggered on a portlet by a user action, and are then communicated to other portlets in order to bring about an indirect change in behavior.

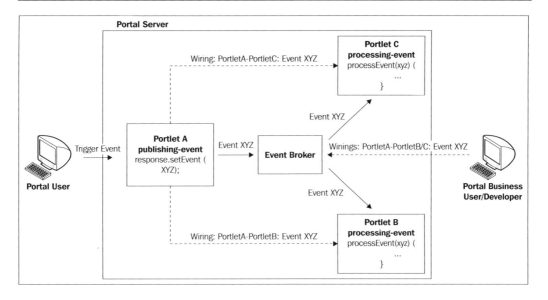

Once we declare that certain portlets can also publish certain events in our deployment descriptor using the `<supported-publishing-event>` tag, a business user, a developer, or a portal administrator can wire various portlets to receive the event using the tag `</supported-processing-event>`. With a good set of re-usable portlets and some creative wiring, we influence a behavior that was probably not even intended by the original portlet developers.

The event broker in the server registers all of the event declarations and the wirings, and brokers all of the requests to the appropriate destinations.

Let us consider our example "MyCompany" portal. We already have a portlet called `DbPortlet`, which we created in an earlier chapter, and that accepts employee ID in order to show the vacation requests. Let's create another simple portlet called `AssetPortlet`, which accepts an employee ID, in order to show the inventory of the office assets owned by the employee. The portlet is pretty straightforward, and uses a couple of JSPs for the initial form page to accept the ID, and the response to list the assets. The code can be found along with the sample code for this chapter.

The `AssetPortlet` is a standalone portlet that functions without any dependencies. However, given that we are already accepting the employee ID for the vacation management portlet, how do we pass this employee ID to the `AssetPortlet`, which refreshes a particular employee's assets along with the pending vacation requests? This can be a pretty realistic example of data being re-used through portlet coordination.

Let's look at each step in detail.

Creating and retrieving events

First, let's add the event code. We will generate the event in DbPortlet and accept the event in AssetPortlet.

Before we generate an event, we need to create an event class that carries the event information. We are using a custom class here, and calling it GenericEvent for demonstration purposes. We can call the class by any name, and can also use primitive types, or any Java class defined by JAXB 2.0. Please note that for passing a single String field, a custom class is overkill; but event classes can be used to carry a large number of variables and values.

```
import java.io.Serializable;
import javax.xml.bind.annotation.XmlRootElement;
import javax.xml.namespace.QName;

@XmlRootElement
public class GenericEvent implements Serializable {
    private static final long serialVersionUID = 1L;
    public static final QName QNAME = new QName
                ("http://www.mycompanyportal.org/ipc", "EmpIdEvent");
    private String empId;
    public String getEmpId() {
        return empId;
    }
    public void setEmpId(String empId) {
        this.empId = empId;
    }
}
```

This is a simple serializable class, and needs to be annotated with @XmlRootElement. We will, therefore, need JAXB library in our build path. JBoss server comes with the jaxb-api.jar class in its lib directory, which can be included in the build classpath. The file also defines an optional public variable called QName that can be used by all portlets, without redefining QName. We have assigned a value to QName, with both a name space and a localPart defining our event.

To publish our event, we edit the DbPortlet file and add the following entry to the processAction method.

```
public void processAction (ActionRequest request,
   ActionResponse actionResponse)
        throws PortletException, java.io.IOException {

...
...
```

```
/* Set event for event-based coordination */
GenericEvent event = new GenericEvent();
event.setEmpId(empId);
actionResponse.setEvent(GenericEvent.QNAME, event );
}
```

We have defined the new event objects and set the variable `empId` as its value. We then added the event to the response, so that the container can now pass it to the subscribers of this event.

In order for the `AssetPortlet` to receive the event, we need to add the following lines of code to the class:

```
...
public void processEvent(EventRequest eventRequest,
    EventResponse response)
    throws PortletException, IOException {
      Event event = eventRequest.getEvent();
      if(event.getQName().equals(GenericEvent.QNAME)) {

          GenericEvent genEvent = (GenericEvent)event.getValue();
          empId = genEvent.getEmpId();
      }
   }
}
...
```

Here, `empId` is declared as a private class variable. The new `processEvent` method implemented by the `GenericPortlet` class, which `AssetPortlet` extends, is added to the `AssetPortlet`, which now receives the event, compares the `QName` of the event with the one we are using, and retrieves the parameter that we are interested in.

It is useful to note that the `processAction` method is not called. This method can still be used for a regular implementation of the portlet.

Next, the container calls the `doView` render method, and we can now easily use the just retrieved value of `empId` to perform the appropriate logic and show the assets page in the `AssetPortlet` window.

Configuring events

All we are left with is to inform the container that the portlets are participating in an inter-portlet communication.

To achieve this, we need to add the following entries to the `portlet.xml`
deployment descriptor:

```
<!-- Event definition for coordination  -->
<event-definition>
    <qname xmlns:mycompany='http://www.mycompanyportal.org/ipc'>
        mycompany:EmpIdEvent
    </qname>
    <value-type>
        org.mycompany.portlet.asset.events.GenericEvent
    </value-type>
</event-definition>
```

The `<event-definition>` tag defines the event, including its QName and the custom
event class that it is declared in. It is a sibling node of the portlet tag, and we can
have many such definitions.

```
<portlet-app>
    ...
    <portlet>
        <portlet-name>DbPortlet</portlet-name>
        <portlet-class>
            org.mycompany.portlet.db.DbPortlet
        </portlet-class>
        ...
        <!-- event-based coordination - event publisher -->
        <supported-publishing-event>
            <qname xmlns:mycompany='http://www.mycompanyportal.org/ipc'>
                mycompany:EmpIdEvent
            </qname>
        </supported-publishing-event>
    </portlet>
    ...
<portlet-app>
```

The `<supported-publishing-event>` tag defines the portlet that generates the
event. In our case, this is the `DbPortlet`, which publishes the `empId` field wrapped in
the `GenericEvent` class.

```
<portlet-app>
    ...
    <portlet>
        <portlet-name>AssetPortlet</portlet-name>
        <portlet-class>
            org.mycompany.portlet.asset.AssetPortlet
        </portlet-class>
        ...
        <!-- event-based coordination - event consumer -->
        <supported-processing-event>
```

```
        <qname xmlns:mycompany='http://www.mycompanyportal.org/ipc'>
            mycompany:EmpIdEvent
        </qname>
    </supported-processing-event>
  </portlet>
  ...
<portlet-app>
```

Similarly, the tag `<supported-processing-event>` denotes the consumer or the processor of the event. In our case, it is `AssetPortlet`, and it consumes the `empId` field in the event class.

We are now ready to package and deploy. The deployment descriptor indicates that both the `DbPortlet` and `AssetPortlet` go in the left column.

```
        <window>
            <window-name>DbPortletWindow</window-name>
            <instance-ref>DbPortletInstance</instance-ref>
            <region>left</region>
            <height>0</height>
        </window>
        <window>
            <window-name>AssetPortletWindow</window-name>
            <instance-ref>AssetPortletInstance</instance-ref>
            <region>left</region>
            <height>1</height>
        </window>
```

Deploying portlets

Once deployed, the default screen looks like the following example, with both portlets highlighted in the left column on their initial default pages:

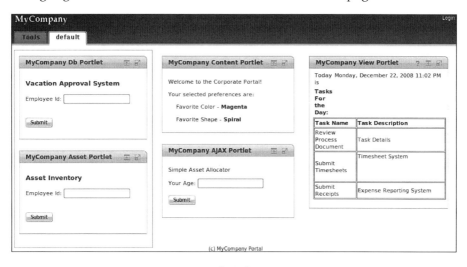

However, once we enter the employee ID in the **Db Portlet** on the top, we see the following result:

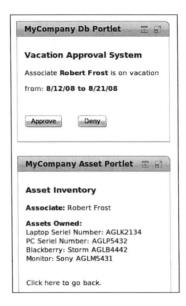

So, we can see that the ID got passed to the **Asset Portlet**, which refreshed its view without any direct interaction with the user, and solely due to coordination with the **Db Portlet**.

It is interesting to further note that the **Asset Portlet** continues to function independently.

Public render parameter-based coordination

We discussed the public render parameter-based coordination before; now let's use it in an example.

We will use the same example that we used in our event-based coordination. Instead of events, we will pass the variable `empId` as a public render parameter. With a single `String` variable being passed between portlets, this is a good use-case for using the public render parameter sharing approach.

Coding public parameters

The code to pass the parameters as public variables and to retrieve them is pretty straightforward.

We need to add the following code to the `DbPortlet`, which is the portlet that gets invoked by the user, and is passed an employee ID:

```
public void processAction (ActionRequest request,
    ActionResponse actionResponse)
    throws PortletException, java.io.IOException {

  . . .

    actionResponse.setRenderParameter("empId", empId);
}
```

All we need to do is to set the parameter `empId` as a `renderParameter` variable in `actionResponse`.

To retrieve the value in `AssetPortlet`, which will then use the parameter to refresh the asset page, we use the regular `renderRequest` class:

```
public void doView(RenderRequest request,RenderResponse response)
      throws PortletException,IOException {
  empId = request.getParameter("empId");
    . . .
}
```

Given that this is a render parameter, we add the `getParameter` call to the `doView` method. The shared render parameter is not retrieved as a regular render parameter.

Configuring public render parameters

So far, nothing is special about the code, but to actually make a parameter a public, shared render parameter, we need to edit `portlet.xml`.

First, we need to define the parameter that we are going to share. This can be done by adding the following code to the `portlet.xml` file as a sibling to the `<portlet>`:

```
<!-- Public Render Parameter-based coordination -->
<public-render-parameter>
    <identifier>empId</identifier>
    <qname xmlns:mycompany='http://www.mycompanyportal.org/ipc'>
        mycompany:EmpId
    </qname>
</public-render-parameter>
```

This declares the variable (as `identifier`) and assigns a `QName` to it.

To make the parameter shared between the two portlets, we need to add the identifier variable to both of the portlet definitions as follows:

```
<portlet>
    <portlet-name>DbPortlet</portlet-name>
    <portlet-class>
        org.mycompany.portlet.db.DbPortlet
    </portlct-class>
    ...
    <!-- Public Render Parameter -->
    <supported-public-render-parameter>
        empId
    </supported-public-render-parameter>
</portlet>
```

This indicates that `DbPortlet` wants to share the parameter `empId` as a public parameter:

```
<portlet>
    <portlet-name>AssetPortlet</portlet-name>
    <portlet-class>
        org.mycompany.portlet.asset.AssetPortlet
    </portlet-class>
    ...
    <!-- Public Render Parameter -->
    <supported-public-render-parameter>
        empId
    </supported-public-render-parameter>
</portlet>
```

Similarly, the same tag definition in `AssetPortlet` identifies that this parameter is shared.

Although used for a single parameter, we can add multiple entries to `portlet.xml`, in order to define multiple parameters.

Deploying portlets

That was it. No events or special methods. Now, when we deploy the application, the result is very similar to the one we saw for the event-based coordination, except in the following ways.

When we submit the form in `DbPortlet`, the URL now displays the variable `empId` as a GET parameter to `AssetPortlet`, indicating that the parameter is now shared across portlets:

```
http://localhost:8080/portal/portal/mycompany/default/AssetPortletWind
ow?action=6&empId=456&mode=view
```

One of the advantages of having the value in the URL is the fact that it can also be bookmarked. As with events, the `AssetPortlet` can continue to function independently as well as in coordination with `DbPortlet`.

Public render parameters are an easy way to implement portlet coordination if our needs are simple, but event-based coordination provides us with an extensive set of options.

Additional JBoss coordination features

Although the JSR-286 specification takes significant strides in terms of providing features for portlet coordination, it still leaves a few scenarios unaddressed. Most of these relate to how portlets behave inside the container. The new portlet specification, as we discussed earlier, provides standards for portal behavior, and leaves the bindings of portlets within the portal up to the portal implementation. This makes the coordination features restrictive, to some extent.

For example:

- When the events are created and wired, we cannot selectively block specific portlets from receiving them. All bound and wired portlets will receive the generated event, unless we redeploy the application with new bindings.

- Similarly, once they are wired, we cannot control when certain portlets receive the render parameters. The parameter with the defined name is shared, and will be retrieved from the `renderRequest` regardless of whether there is a local parameter with the same name, that we want to use for a use-case.

- It is possible that portlets may have to use both events and render parameters. There is a possibility that, although syntactically different, they might have the same values semantically. The specification establishes no relationship between shared render parameters and events.

JBoss Portal Server 2.7.0 extends the coordination model and addresses these through a concept of "Implicit" and "Explicit" wirings. By providing a granular level of control over wirings and bindings, the server further opens up a vast array of mix-and-match options when dealing with events and render parameters for coordination.

JBoss portal server doesn't treat events and shared parameters differently. Both of them are configured similarly, with a QName and using "Event Binding" options for events and "Parameter Bindings" for public/shared render parameters.

Implicit and explicit coordination

The default behavior, as defined by the specification, with portlet bindings and wirings defined in deployment descriptors using a shared QName, is termed as implicit coordination. In this type of behavior, the behavior is implicit and predetermined by the specification as long as the wirings and bindings are defined appropriately. This is the default behavior in JBoss portal server, and the examples that we have seen earlier demonstrate implicit behavior.

However, if we do not want the default behavior, but want to add some other controls on how bindings and wirings are configured, then JBoss offers custom coordination extensions, and categorizes them as explicit coordination. These bindings and wirings are configured in either the proprietary *-object.xml deployment descriptor, or by using the administrative console. Once the behavior is set to explicit coordination, the default implicit state is overridden.

Explicit coordination configuration

Explicit coordination parameters are configured in the *-object.xml file, using a special tag called <coordination>. Its general structure appears as follows:

```
<portal>
...
  <coordination>
  <bindings>
     <implicit-mode>FALSE</implicit-mode>
       <alias-binding>
         ..
       </alias-binding>
  </bindings>
   </wirings>
    <implicit-mode>FALSE</implicit-mode>
   <wirings>
  </coordination>
</portal>
```

As stated earlier, coordination can also be configured from the administrative console. There is new link on the parameters page called **Coordination** that takes us to the page coordination configuration page. The three sections, **Events**, **Parameters**, and **Bindings** can be collapsed for easy reading. Also, by default, this page doesn't show any entries, even if we have coordination defined in `portlet.xml`. This is because the events and shared parameters need to be defined in `*-object.xml`, the JBoss deployment descriptor.

Explicit coordination can currently be configured only at the page level.

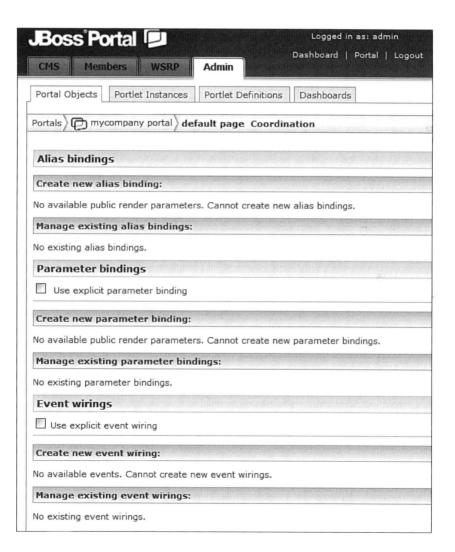

Let us understand this a little better with our example. Let's say we want to disable all wirings temporarily, but keep the bindings for the values that are being shared. All we have to do is add the following entry to `*-object.xml`:

```
<portal>
 <page>
...
   <coordination>
     <bindings>
        <implicit-mode>TRUE</implicit-mode>
       <parameter-binding>
          ...
       </parameter-binding>
       <alias-binding>
          ...
       </alias-binding>
     </bindings>
     <wirings>
       <implicit-mode>FALSE</implicit-mode>
       <event-wiring>
          ...
       </event-wiring>
     </wirings>
   </coordination>
     ...
 </page>
</portal>
```

Alternatively, we can select the **Use explicit event wiring** checkbox in the **Events Wirings** section. For disabling the values shared, but to keep the wirings, we can edit the configuration in a similar manner, and set the `<implicit-mode>` for `<bindings>` to FALSE.

Let's look at the explicit coordination features in a bit more detail, with specific scenarios.

Event wiring

To manage wirings using the explicit coordination option, we need to first register our events, sources, and destination. The following code snippet, which is added to the `*-object.xml` descriptor, creates the entries in the coordination screen that we saw earlier. We have already established the wirings in the configuration, but we will shortly see how we can manage these wirings.

```
<portal>
  <page>
     ...
    <coordination>
       ...
      <wirings>
```

```
            <implicit-mode>FALSE</implicit-mode>
            <event-wiring>
                <name>EmpIdEventWiring</name>
                  <sources>
                    <window-coordination>
                      <window-name>DbPortletWindow</window-name>
                      <qname>{urn:mycompany}EmpIdEvent</qname>
                    </window-coordination>
                  </sources>
                  <destinations>
                    <window-coordination>
                      <window-name>AssetPortletWindow</window-name>
                      <qname>{urn:mycompany}EmpIdEvent</qname>
                    </window-coordination>
                    <window-coordination>
                      <window-name>ViewPortletWindow</window-name>
                      <qname>{urn:mycompany}EmpIdEvent</qname>
                    </window-coordination>
                  </destinations>
            </event-wiring>
          </wirings>
        </coordination>
      </page>
       . . .
  </portal>
```

This configuration is pretty straightforward. The `<coordination>` node declared for a portal page houses the `<wirings>` node, which in turn, lists the event sources and destinations, along with their common wiring parameters, which are defined in QName.

Once deployed, the console screen appears as follows:

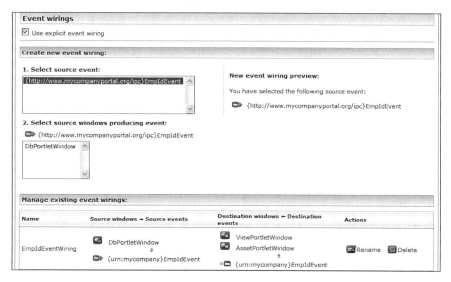

We can see our source event, the windows it originates from, and the destination windows that will consume the event. Now, if we want to redefine our wirings, we have to start a small multi-step selection process, beginning with selecting the source window the event gets produced from. This will refresh the screen to present the destination event, and eventually the destination window. Once we select the destination window, the event will be a consumer, we can complete our wiring and give it a name.

The panel on the right provides the status of the flow. In our example, we have a single window and a single event, but imagine a typical enterprise portal where there are many windows and events, and the options that explicit event wirings offer, in terms of combinations, can be very powerful.

Parameter binding

Parameter binding defines the render parameters that are shared across multiple portlets. We can bind parameters between portlets by using the following configuration snippet:

```
<portal>
 <page>
      . . .
   <coordination>
       <bindings>
         <implicit-mode>FALSE</implicit-mode>
          <parameter-binding>
            <id>EmpidParameterBinding</id>
```

```
    <window-coordination>
        <window-name>DbPortletWindow</window-name>
        <qname>empId</qname>
    </window-coordination>
    <window-coordination>
        <window-name>AssetPortletWindow</window-name>
        <qname>empId</qname>
    </window-coordination>
    <window-coordination>
        <window-name>ViewPortletWindow</window-name>
        <qname>{urn:mycompany}EmpIdEvent</qname>
    </window-coordination>
    </parameter-binding>
  </bindings>
 </coordination>
 </page>
  . . .
</portal>
```

Not only we can share render parameters and semantically-equivalent parameters that carry the same value, but we can actually integrate them in an event. As JBoss portal treats both the render parameters and the events in the same way, it is also possible for us to bind parameters that are generated by events. This allows us to be flexible in integrating with the other portlets in the enterprise that might not readily share the same coordination model.

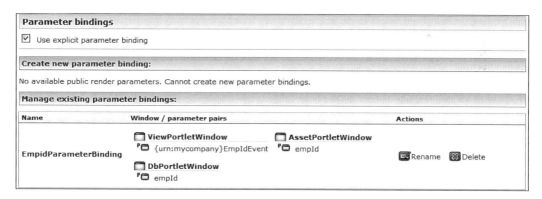

In our case, we can see that in the administrative user interface, the configuration created entries for explicit parameter-based coordination, and the parameters involved, are not just empId but an event {urn:mycompany}EmpIdEvent from our previous event configuration. As we add more public parameters, we should be able to create new bindings using the upper segment of the user interface.

Alias binding

Alias binding is a JBoss portal-specific configuration that helps us to provide an alias to variables that are semantically alike. In our example, the public render parameter `empId` and the event object `EmpIdEvent` carry the same employee identifier information. Given that we can use these interchangeably, using explicit bindings, Alias binding offers a way to assign a common alias to both.

The following configuration entry shows how the alias is configured:

```
<portal>
 <page>
      . . .
   <coordination>
       <bindings>
          <implicit-mode>FALSE</implicit-mode>
        <alias-binding>
           <id>emplid</id>
             <qname>empId</qname>
        </alias-binding>
        <alias-binding>
           <id>employeeId</id>
             <qname>empId</qname>
             <qname>{urn:mycompany}EmpIdEvent</qname>
        </alias-binding>
            . . .
       </bindings>
   </coordination>
 </page>
      . . .
</portal>
```

The `<alias-binding>` node is a child of the `<bindings>` node, and it can be used to configure an alias for a single `QName`, or to club multiple names together.

The user interface reflects the configurations, as shown in the following screenshot:

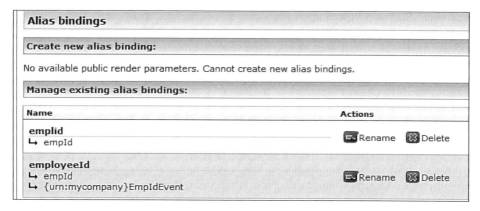

If more public render parameters are added to the application, they will be visible in the upper segment of the user interface for us to manually configure the aliases.

Explicit coordination greatly enhances the coordination capabilities prescribed by the Portlet 2.0 specification. We can define implicit coordination as a default, by declaring `<implicit-mode>TRUE</implicit-mode>` at the portal level, but we can override them at the page-level for specific behavior.

Portlet filters

One of the other major features included in the Portlet 2.0 specification is the ability to add filters to portlets. Filters are Java classes that are used to modify requests and responses before and after the life cycle method of a portlet is invoked.

Portlet filters behave in the same manner as a servlet filter except for one major difference. Servlet handles requests only with a single method, `service()`. Hence, there is only a single type of servlet filter that wraps around the method processing. However, there are four life cycle methods in portlet filters, resulting in four types of Portlet filters.

The specification defines the following methods:

1. `javax.portlet.filter.ActionFilter`: Filters requests to `processAction` method.
2. `javax.portlet.filter.RenderFilter`: Filters requests to `render` method.
3. `javax.portlet.filter.ResourceFilter`: Filters requests to `serveResource` method.
4. `javax.portlet.filter.EventFilter`: Filters requests to `processEvent` method.

The structure of a typical filter looks like this:

```
public class SomePortletFilter implements EventFilter {
    public void doFilter(EventRequest eventRequest, EventResponse
    eventResponse, FilterChain filterChain) throws IOException,
    PortletException {
        . . .
        . . .
}

public void destroy() {
        // some resource release activities
}

public void init(FilterConfig arg0) throws PortletException {
        // initialize values
}
```

Each filter type extends the base `PortletFilter` class and inherits the `init()` and `destroy()` methods. The `init` method provides access to the `FilterConfig`, where initial values can be set in the deployment descriptor. The `doFilter` method forms the core of the filter class and, depending on the type of life cycle method the filter is mapped to, the parameters change accordingly.

For example, for the `processEvent` method, the parameters are `EventRequest` and `EventResponse`. Similarly, for the `processAction` method, the parameters that will be passed to `doFilter` are `ActionRequest` and `ActionResponse`. Filters can also be chained together.

The `doFilter` method can create custom request and response objects to be passed to the life cycle methods, by using the `RequestWrapper` and `ResponseWrapper` classes. However, care should be taken to follow the best practices for writing wrapper classes, only overwriting existing methods, and not creating new ones as it is not known if there are more filters in the chain.

To create a portlet filter, we need to follow these steps:

1. Write a filter class with the appropriate life cycle method and portlet in mind. Here, we need to decide on the kind of behavior that we want to inject either before or after the portlet life cycle method is executed.

2. Define the filter in the deployment descriptor `portlet.xml`.

3. Map the filter to the appropriate portlet.

Let's walk thorough these steps using an example.

We want to implement a simple authorization check in the ViewPortlet that we built earlier. All this does is authenticate a user and either provide or deny access to the ViewPortlet for this user.

Creating the filter

We want the portlet to either display content, or give an error message based on the user. Hence, we will create a RenderFilter method that deals with how the view is rendered to the user.

The code looks like this:

```
public class ViewPortletFilter implements RenderFilter {
   public void doFilter(RenderRequest renderRequest, RenderResponse
   renderResponse, FilterChain filterChain) throws IOException,
   PortletException {
       // before mapped portlet is invoked
       // the filter implements a simple security check based on
          authenticated user
       String user = renderRequest.getRemoteUser();
       if (user != null && user.equals("user")) {
         renderRequest.setAttribute("user","Unauthorized");
         PrintWriter writer = renderResponse.getWriter();
         writer.write("<font color=red> Unauthorized <font>");
                 writer.close();
       } else {
           // go on to the portlet this filter maps
           filterChain.doFilter(renderRequest, renderResponse);
           // after mapped portlet is done executing the render method
           System.out.println("After Portlet");
           // add some information that is not required to be
             hardcoded in the portlet
           renderRequest.setAttribute("announcement","Note: Accounts
                                  close early this week!");
       }
   }
    public void destroy() {
       // some resource release activities
    }
    public void init(FilterConfig arg0) throws PortletException {
       // initialize values
    }
}
```

The doFilter method retrieves the user information and, if the user is unauthorized, doesn't proceed further with the execution of the render method, instead replacing it with a text. Otherwise, the method gets executed as usual.

Also, after the method has been executed, the filter adds a request variable with an announcement. The view JSP just needs a placeholder, whereas the announcement can be automatically added to the final view. This can be very useful when we don't want to change the portlet behavior.

Configuring the filter

Filters are defined in `portlet.xml` as follows:

```
<!-- filter declaration -->
  <filter>
    <filter-name>ViewPortletFilter</filter-name>
    <filter-class>
        org.mycompany.portlet.filter.ViewPortletFilter
    </filter-class>
    <lifecycle>RENDER_PHASE</lifecycle>
  </filter>
```

We define the name of the filter, the class that implements the filter, and the life cycle method that we want to use with the filter. Other options are ACTION_PHASE, EVENT_PHASE, and RESOURCE_PHASE.

Mapping the filter

The filter is mapped to the appropriate portlet as follows:

```
<!-- filter mapping   -->
<filter-mapping>
  <filter-name>ViewPortletFilter</filter-name>
  <portlet-name>ViewPortlet</portlet-name>
</filter-mapping>
```

The mapping is pretty straightforward, using the filter name that we defined earlier in the filter definition, and the portlet name that we defined in the portlet definition.

Deployment

The filter gets packaged in the same way as any other class, and once deployed on the server, we can test to see if our functionality works.

After the portal page loads, if we are not authenticated, we should be able to see all of the portlets on the page, including the **View Portlet** in the right-hand column. Now, let's go ahead and log in as the user, **user**, because that's how we have defined our filter.

Now, when we try to go to the home page, we see an error, as shown in the following screenshot. This verifies that the filter is intercepting the render method and is executing its own added logic.

We took a very simple example to illustrate portlet filters. The example is neither comprehensive nor indicative of the immense capabilities of filters. There are innumerable possibilities, where filters for each of the life cycle methods can be used extensively, to provide rich portal functionality.

Summary

One of the major complaints with the older JSR-168 specification was the lack of support for inter-portlet communication. Portlet 2.0 provides a comprehensive set of options to perform robust portlet coordination using events, as well as public parameters. Portlet coordination tremendously increases the capabilities of the portals and portlets by opening up possibilities for integrating not only within the application, but also with other applications within the enterprise. Like web mashups, portlet coordination empowers users to conceive ideas and solutions that were not even foreseen when the portlets were originally built. Filters were long overdue in the specification. However, the granular control portlet filters make them far more powerful than servlet filters.

Epilogue

We have come a long way since we began talking about portals. JBoss portal is one of the most feature-rich portal servers, and provides the whole gamut of capabilities that help developers to build powerful portal applications. It was the first server to offer support for the JSR-286 specification, and continues to break new ground in terms of features and functionality.

In this book we have covered all of the major features of the JBoss portal server, and have discussed all of the aspects that are required when building a strong portal application. We've covered all of the topics, with examples for better understanding of the concepts. The examples were by no means comprehensive; but they were intended to provide enough guidance to build advanced functionality. All of the sample code can be downloaded from the book's web site.

It was fun writing this book, and I hope you enjoyed reading as much as I enjoyed writing it.

Thanks, and happy coding!

Index

I

IDE 41
identity management
  API 194
  identity portlets 190, 191
  users managing, admin console used 189
  ways 189
identity portlets
  CAPTCHA support 191, 192
  configuring 193
  identity management portlet 190
  lost password feature, enabling 192
  reset password feature, enabling 192
  user portlet 190
  user registration, jBPM-based 193
IFrames 107
implementing, AJAX
  in JBoss portal 110, 111
  XMLHttpRequest used 108-110
implicit coordination 238
installing, JBoss portal server
  JBoss portal, building from source 28
  JBoss portal and application server bundle
    23, 24
  JBoss portal binary, without server 25-28
  overview 21
  system requirements 22
Integrated Development Environment. See
    IDE
inter-portlet communication
  and portlet coordination 220, 221
  portlet events 221, 222
  public render parameters 223, 224
interceptors, CMS 163-165
intranet portal
  JSP portlet 69-76
  MyCompany portal, creating 67, 68
  sample application, building 66

J

J2EE servlet
  and portlets, differentiating 17, 18
JACC 179
Jackrabbit 148
Java Authorization Contract for Containers.
    See JACC

Java Business Process Management. See
    jBPM
Java portlet specification
  JSR-168 17, 38, 39
  JSR-286 17, 39
Java Server Faces
  about 61
  application, building 65
  application, deploying 65, 66
  application descriptors 62-64
  JSR -301 portlet bridge 61
  package structure 62
Java Server Pages
  application, building 59
  application, deploying 60, 61
  application descriptors 58, 59
  archive package structure 54
  code, writing 54, 55
  JSPs and portlet tags 57, 58
  portlet class, code 55-57
  using 54
Java Specification Request. See JSR-168
Java Specification Request. See JSR-286
Java Virtual Machine (JVM) 22
JBoss Applicatin Server (AS) bundle 23, 24
JBoss Application Server (AS) 4.2.3 22
JBoss coordination features, portlet
    coordination
  about 237
  alias, binding 244, 245
  event, wiring 240-242
  explicit coordination, configuration
    238, 240
  Implicit and explicit coordination 238
  parameter, binding 242-244
JBoss EAP 4.3 22
JBoss Enterprise Application Platform
    (EAP) 4.2 22
JBoss portal
  2.7.0 version used 20
  access control 177
  AJAX 107
  authentication 177
  authorization 179
  CAS 187-189
  content management system (CMS),
    security 195, 196

N

NORMAL, window state 40

O

Object Relationship Management.
 See ORM
ORM 129

P

personalization 77
personalization content, portals
  access-level based portlets 97, 98
  analytics-based portlets 99
  preferences-based portlets 98, 99
personalization interface, portals
  about 80, 81
  custom development 93, 94
  header.jsp, modifying 94, 95
  JSPs, creating 95, 96
  layout JSP tags, using 84
  layouts 81, 82
  layouts, configuring 85, 86
  layouts, creating 82, 84
  RenderSets 89
  RenderSets, using 89-93
  tabs.jsp, modifying 96
  themes 86
  themes, configuring 87-89
  themes, defining 87
personalization models, portals
  about 79
  collaborative filtering 80
  rules-based 79
  user profile-based 79
personalizing, portals
  personalization content 96, 97
  personalization interface 80, 81
  personalization models 79
portal architecture
  components 13
  content management and publishing 14
  diagrammatic representation 13
  integration interfaces 14
  portlet integration 14
  security 14

user interface 13
portal object, security
  configuration files, used 172-177
  management console, used 170-172
portal page
  about 15, 31, 33, 37
  components 37
  creating 33
portals
  about 7, 15
  architecture, for enterprise 13
  benefits 9
  CMS 148
  content, managing 147
  customizing 99
  features 8
  first portal page 33-35
  function-based portals 9
  getting started 31-33
  internationalization (I18N) 103
  localization (L10N) 103
  need for 8
  personalization content 96, 97
  personalization interface 80, 81
  personalization models 79
  personalizing 78
  portal servers 13
  presentation tier 53
  specification 17
  types 9
  Web Services for Remote Portlets (WSRP)
    specification 17
  working with 31
portal security 169
portal servers
  about 13
  enterprise, portal architecture 13
  J2EE servlet 17
  portal, specification 17
  remoting in 199
  view, constructing 16
  Web Services for Remote Portlets (WSRP)
    17
portlet, building
  Java Server Faces (JSF) used 61, 62
  Java Server Pages (JSP) used 54-58
  JBoss Seam used 66

Business Process Management with JBoss jBPM

ISBN: 978-1-847192-36-3   Paperback: 300 pages

Develop business process models for implementation in a business process management system.

1. Map your business processes in an efficient, standards-friendly way

2. Use the jBPM toolset to work with business process maps, create a customizable user interface for users to interact with the process, collect process execution data, and integrate with existing systems.

3. Set up business rules, assign tasks, work with process variables, automate activities and decisions.

Java EE 5 Development with NetBeans 6

ISBN: 978-1-847195-46-3   Paperback: 384 pages

Develop professional enterprise Java EE applications quickly and easily with this popular IDE

1. Use features of the popular NetBeans IDE to improve Java EE development

2. Careful instructions and screenshots lead you through the options available

3. Covers the major Java EE APIs such as JSF, EJB 3 and JPA, and how to work with them in NetBeans

4. Covers the NetBeans Visual Web designer in detail

Please check **www.PacktPub.com** for information on our titles

EJB 3 Developer Guide

ISBN: 978-1-847195-60-9   Paperback: 259 pages

A Practical Guide for developers and architects to the Enterprise Java Beans Standard

1. A rapid introduction to the features of EJB 3

2. EJB 3 features explored concisely with accompanying code examples

3. Easily enhance Java applications with new, improved Enterprise Java Beans

OpenCms 7 Development

ISBN: 978-1-847191-05-2   Paperback: 292 pages

Extending and customizing OpenCms through its Java API

1. Targets version 7 of OpenCms

2. Create new modules to extend OpenCms functionality

3. Learn to use the OpenCms templating system

Please check **www.PacktPub.com** for information on our titles

2008330